BEAUTY BEYOND THE THORNS

9/18/2022

Jay & Katherine,

I am so grateful to know you from a distance. You have poured hope into my life & I pray to do the same for others. May the words within this book provide hope & healing for you in some way.

In His Beauty,

Darin J. Steiner &

BEAUTY BEYOND

THE

THORNS

DISCOVERING GIFTS
IN SUFFERING

DARCI J. STEINER, MS

ENDORSEMENTS

"Darci has written a book laced with hope and courage and tenacity. She reminds us of the backwards economy of Jesus where the weak are the strong and those who sometimes feel left behind will lead us."

—BOB GOFF
Lawyer, speaker, and author of the *New York Times* best-selling books *Love Does; Everybody, Always*; and *Dream Big*

"When Darci first walked into the vitamin store I was helping to manage, 20 odd years ago, looking for help for her pain, neither of us realized the journey of darkness and healing into light we were about to embark upon together. This book, which chronicles many of the spiritual aspects of that journey, is a powerfully moving and deeply personal addition to *the best* of the spiritual literature on pain and suffering. Most of us struggle with the question of how and why a good God can allow deep loss and painful suffering in the people who cry out to Him in anguish and despair. *Beauty Beyond the Thorns* suggests answers, as it reveals deep transformation in the heart and soul of a courageous woman who refuses to give up."

—CHRISTINA VESELAK, MS, LMFT, CN
Licensed Marriage and Family Therapist and Certified Nutritionist

"I love the content of *Beauty Beyond the Thorns*—it's a wonderful mix of intellectually stimulating information, theologically inspiring exegesis, personal stories, and incredible poetry. I believe this book would be an incredible blessing to anyone who wants to walk with Jesus every day. I can only begin to imagine the impact it would have on someone who deals with chronic pain or significant tragedy."

—PHIL VAUGHAN
Lead Follower, Castle Oaks Covenant Church,
Castle Rock, CO

"A journey through time, culture, pain, and the divine stories found within them all, Darci Joy Steiner's unique devotional is one to be savored slowly. Each chapter in *Beauty Beyond the Thorns: Discovering Gifts in Suffering* is filled with perspective that can only come from one who has walked out the reality of each title. You'll not find shallow platitudes; rather, you'll be deeply encouraged in your own journey of faith to see God's presence in rich and meaningful ways."

—RONNE ROCK
Mentor, storyteller, and author of *One Woman Can Change the World:
Reclaiming Your God-Designed Influence and Impact Right Where You Are*

"Within the pages of *Beauty Beyond the Thorns: Discovering Gifts in Suffering* you'll be taken on a journey to find hope in the most unexpected places. Darci Steiner shares truth that is often hidden by our own experiences of pain. But her words and personal story will help you to find what God may want to do with your story as well."

—DON TALLEY
Associate VP, Youth for Christ USA

What a gift to experience *Beauty Beyond the Thorns*. This is not just a book, but a delicate, candid, and vulnerable unveiling of the healing journey that pain and suffering offers—an invitation to transformation. Darci has pulled back the curtain and humbly allowed a glimpse into the heart, the wrestling, the anguish, the faith, acceptance, and fortitude it takes to truly surrender to the path God lays out before us when we endure affliction.

If you are willing to embark on this journey, Darci will illuminate spiritual truths, and deep wells of God's wisdom and love for you. You will see your precious connection to His story. As you hear her written voice, feel the emotion of her poetry, and see how these align with the Word of God, you will have the opportunity to embrace joy amidst your trials, lay bare your questions, strengthen your resilience, and see freedom and hope even in agony and distress.

If you are hurting, or if you know and love someone who is, this is for you. If you want to deepen your walk with God as you travel through this broken world, this is for you. As one who has counseled people for nearly 25 years, this book will be a go-to on my Christian therapist's shelf!

—DR. TRACY JONES, Ed.D, LPC, LMHC
Licensed Professional Counselor and Licensed Mental Health
Counselor

"Darci has an excellent and rare presence as an author. She is beautifully honest, humble, and powerful. Her beauty lies in the calmness of her tone while discussing earth-shattering revelations about God and suffering. Truly, I wish I had had *Beauty Beyond the Thorns* to read when I went through the last 5 years of my own life. Steiner's premise is while she previously went through tragedy and pain, she realized good DID come from it. To now be suffering again, Darci is almost suffering with excitement for what God is trying to teach her. It's astounding."

—KASSIDI SIKES
Manuscript Editor

"Darci Steiner perfectly blends the Bible with the triumphs and tragedies of everyday life in her book, *Beauty Beyond the Thorns*. Every chapter of leaves you longing for the next, to see how spirituality and the human spirit can work together to make the world a better place. A must-read for your soul!"

—GREGORY NIETO
Reporter, Channel 2 & FOX31 Denver

"Do you feel like the thorns in your life are only ugly and negative? Though they are indeed painful, you can learn to see them as gifts instead of burdens. Through hard-won truths, Darci shares authentic stories of her own, others and Bible characters to show how beautiful and valuable our hard times can be. You'll learn how to view your difficulties in new ways as you read, and it is as enjoyable as sitting down to have coffee with Darci."

—SARAH GERINGER
Author of *Transforming Your Thought Life: Christian Meditation in Focus* and *Transforming Your Thought Life for Teens: Renew Your Mind with God*

"In this moving and very personal book, Darci Steiner allows the wisdom of scripture to be refracted through the prism of her own suffering. Even in the midst of pain, she finds gifts from God everywhere in her experience, and she has written in this volume a testament that is itself a gift to all who read it."

—THOMAS G. LONG
Bandy Professor Emeritus of Preaching, Candler School of Theology, Emory University, author of *What Shall We Say: Evil Suffering and the Crisis of Faith*

For Mark.
I look into your eyes, down into your soul,
and I see a glimpse into what heaven will be like.
I love you!

Study Guide for Beauty Beyond the Thorns: Discovering Gifts in Suffering
Available on Amazon!

If you don't yet have a copy of the *Study Guide for Beauty Beyond the Thorns: Discovering Gifts in Suffering*, I'd encourage you to get one to work alongside the book. You can use the book and study guide in a variety of ways:

1. With a Bible study group, support group, any group, or book club
2. By yourself at your own pace
3. With a friend or two
4. With a spouse or partner

Since there are thirty chapters, you can study one chapter per day for a month. If you are working through the book and study guide with a group that meets weekly, each member can study one chapter per day, then at your weekly meeting discuss the chapters read that week. You can use these books in any way that work best for your situation. I pray these books provide you with healing.

Website: www.DarciJSteiner.com

CONTENTS

PROLOGUE

Ascending Longs Peak

I can see most of the front range of the Colorado Rocky Mountains from our back deck. It's why we chose this house. I sit on the deck frequently because I can take only a few steps per day. I watch the hawks soar against the sky, and sometimes, they swoop in on a vole or a snake and stop for lunch atop a nearby Douglas fir to rip apart and enjoy their delicacy. Lifting my gaze beyond the pine tree, I marvel at the view of my favorite mountain, Longs Peak. The majesty it projects astounds me every time I behold its beauty. It is so rugged, so pronounced. My eyes scan the other Colorado fourteeners, and they are breathtaking as well. But Longs Peak and I have a bond.

You see, I am a long sufferer. I've metaphorically been climbing Longs Peak since I was eighteen, when my health issues began with chronic migraines. My ascent has lasted nearly forty years, various ailments keeping me from reaching its summit. But I persevere day after day, putting one foot in front of the other. Why am I headed to the summit of this majestic peak? Because it's where we're all headed. All of us are on a journey to attain, accomplish, achieve, or experience something.

I didn't choose Longs Peak; it chose me. I would have chosen Mt. Bierstadt, Grays, or Torreys, summitted by noon, and returned safely before the dangers of afternoon lightning. On my ascent, I have almost died. People die on Longs Peak regularly due to falls or "exposure."[1] I've been told I'm feisty, and God has used feisty in me to help keep me alive. Day by day, I get closer to the summit. I have not a step to waste.

Suffering is something we all encounter, and when lightning strikes, we realize we aren't in control of our fate. We journey through trials because if we give up, we'd die from exposure. As we press onward, up the rugged trail, our journey provides growth for us along the way. Before we know it, we have gained greater joy, deeper compassion, profound peace, or tenacious courage. We turn around to look at the view and realize it is becoming increasingly magnificent. We reach a summit every day—not *the* summit, but a summit of sorts. Why do we do this? I do it because I have a purpose—a God-given purpose—and my Longs Peak is helping me attain it.

I also have someone by my side, grabbing my hand when I feel I can't go on. He carries me every day when I get too weary. He sees my suffering and understands because he climbed up to Golgotha carrying a heavy wooden cross. Raise your hand if you've been crucified for the sins of the world? I didn't think so. Whose pain has been worse than that? My Savior can relate, so I've invited him into my suffering journey so he can help me. He embodies the gear I need—courage, perseverance, direction, and a refuge from the storm. He gifts me characteristics of himself to help me endure the climb. I can't make it alone, so I trek with him. Step by step, day by day, I climb my Longs Peak, even though I can't walk.

I don't know when I'll reach the final summit, but when I do, I will have reached my goal—heaven. I "Run in such a way as to get the prize ... to get a crown that will last forever" (1 Cor. 9:24–25). I'm in this for the long haul until my God-given purpose is fulfilled. Until then, I turn around on the trail to enjoy the view from the heights I've attained. It's beautiful. Would you believe me if I told you we can suffer and experience joy at the same time? Have you felt delight even while your muscles are burning during a climb? Is elation felt alongside the pains of childbirth? Can a mountain be simultaneously majestic and rugged? Joy and suffering can co-exist in the same space; they can be experienced together.

The greatest gift of love the world has ever known—Jesus dying on a cross—was unwrapped through suffering. *Beauty Beyond the Thorns: Discovering Gifts in Suffering* is a guidebook filled with similar paradoxes that reveal however long your suffering journey, there are gifts to attain along the way; they are characteristics God himself embraces.

SHARE IN HIS SUFFERINGS

The Bible is filled with mystery and paradoxical concepts. God invites us to share in his sufferings so we can also share in his blessings (Rom. 8:17). We need to view our lives a bit differently if we are to understand this concept. As Bob Goff brilliantly states: "It was a backward economy Jesus talked about. He said if people wanted to be at the front of the line, they needed to go to the back. If they wanted to be a good leader, they would need to be an even better follower. If they wanted to know Him better, they'd need to stop thinking so much about themselves, and if they wanted to love Him more, they needed to love each other more."[2]

God may even use our suffering to provide gifts to those around us. When the bleeding woman reached out in faith to touch the fringe of Jesus' cloak, he not only healed her, but—those watching in the crowd found healing for *their* faithlessness and hopelessness. (Luke 8:48).

We all need healing, whether we're experiencing physical or emotional pain from the thorns of divorce, job loss, grief, abuse, addiction, infertility, disability, financial troubles—any trouble. When we follow Jesus, God offers gifts such as hope, compassion, and mercy to help us through trials. It seems we turn to God most often when we are in distress—when we are desperate, we realize there is nowhere else to go. As author Jen Oshman says, "God often gives us way more than we're comfortable with so that we might cry out to him."[3] During tribulation, God shows his power most profoundly, as you will see exemplified in each story of this book.

Sometimes, we learn best from our life experiences, but failing to learn lessons from the lives of others, is like staying in a house caught on fire because you've never been burned. You don't have to wait to learn to get out of a burning house until you are stuck in one—you get out because you have learned from other people who haven't been as fortunate.

The goal I have in writing this book and its companion, *Study Guide for Beauty Beyond the Thorns* is to provide aha moments for you through stories of forgiveness and healing, pain and joy, struggle and victory, love and redemption, and hopelessness and hope. You will laugh, maybe cry, and resonate with the serious, profound, and funny. If you aren't a follower of Jesus, please stay for the climb. Many people Jesus healed were not believers. He is compassionate toward everyone and heals each of us in various ways. You are welcome here.

The healings Jesus performed in the Bible provide the backbone of *Beauty Beyond the Thorns* because they address physical, mental, emotional, and spiritual healing. Modern-day stories of suffering are paralleled with biblical accounts of healing that will both enrich your understanding of the Bible and provide hope for your personal journey.

My promise to you is lofty: After reading this book and working through the Study Guide, you will view and experience suffering differently. Each chapter will provide insight as to how God uses suffering to form you and deepen your relationship with him. It is within suffering that God reveals himself to you just like he revealed himself to the world at the cross. Suffering provides opportunities for you to understand the sufferings of Jesus and draw closer to him. The cross is where darkness and light meet. When you feel you are in the dark, you will find love and hope at the cross.

I hope you will turn to these pages repeatedly to help you find loving benefits God reveals during painful seasons. Pull this book out like a compass to help you find meaning and purpose in suffering and point you back to God—True North. Remember, God uses our pain to reflect his story to the world.

"While the world has always worshipped strength, God chose weakness to display his love."[4] I am physically weak, but God strengthens me to balance the scale. May these pages point you toward the Healer so you can find healing in your pain. You are not alone. Whether your suffering is short or long, he is your refuge from the storm. Jesus—he is the beauty beyond our thorns.

CHAPTER 1

The Gift of Hope – My Journey

How can we understand hope without having faith?

CHILDREN

When my daughters were born in 1995 and 1998, I was so excited to have kids my heart would not stop racing. My doctor diagnosed me with "post-partum elation." Every day was an adventure going to the zoo, library, park, aquarium, and sports camps. The girls and I loved to cuddle, make forts, and eat hot dogs in igloos we created in the Colorado snow. My most cherished desire in life with my husband Mark was children. Our dreams had come true.

THE YEAR 2000

"Mommy, are you okay?" five-year-old Jenny asked sweetly, standing above me while I lay stunned on the floor. Two-and-a-half-year-old Nicole came and plopped down beside me.

My fall happened so fast. I ran up the stairs to get a CD, but as I turned to run back down, I slipped on a piece of paper, began tumbling, and couldn't regain my footing. By the time I reached the lower steps, I was upright again, so I hurdled (and almost hurled) over the baby gate set up across the bottom step. I slammed into the wall, which tossed and twisted me in the opposite direction where I face-planted onto the floor. The baby-gate remained fully intact. However, my body did not.

I didn't know it then, but my back injury from the fall would land me a two-year, full-time job in bed. While confined to bed, I developed a nerve pain disorder called Complex Regional Pain Syndrome, or CRPS. Most people who develop CRPS never heal from it—it is complex and excruciatingly painful. The syndrome is uncommon and usually initiated by an injury. The pain from CRPS is out of proportion to the injury. In other words, my injured nerves sent signals to my brain that made me extremely sensitive to pain, unlike what a person without the syndrome would feel. My pain spiraled out of control, rendering me unable to function normally.

Depression was my next malady.

THE YEAR 2002

As I lay on my side in bed, I listen to my sweet family eat dinner downstairs. I hear the gentle clanking of forks against porcelain plates while Mark and the girls enjoy a meal together. I gently pull my knees to my chest and lay in the fetal position. Tears flow onto my pillow, dampening the left side of my face. "Where are you, God? I don't feel you. Do you see me? How did my life get to this place?"

My pain is unbearable even on OxyContin and a myriad of other medications. As I lay there, I stare at the array of orange medicine bottles on the nightstand. I want to die as much as I want to live. I have always been intensely in love with my husband and little girls; I love our life, but I don't know how to keep enduring this agony day after day, year after year. "If you can do anything, God, why won't you heal me?" It's not just the physical torment I feel, but the gut-wrenching heartache. I yearn to hold the girls tight, go to their soccer games, and push them on swings at the park.

I weigh a hundred pounds. Muscles throughout my body are atrophied, including my cheeks and I cannot even smile. However, I can wrap my middle finger and thumb around my lower leg and upper arms. My bone mass is minimal—I have osteopenia. Pain depletes hunger and the thought of food makes me sick, sick, sick.

Mark comes up the stairs to run the bathwater, and the girls hop in the tub with their little plastic sea creatures. Their laughter lightens my spirit, but the burden of not being with them drowns out the positivity. There is nothing I want more than to participate in life with my family.

As the water drains from the tub, my little girls, wrapped in their purple dinosaur towels, run to the side of the bed to kiss me goodnight. Not one kiss is taken for granted. Oh, how I miss holding and embracing them. The girls race back downstairs to watch *The Lion King* while their daddy carefully combs their long blonde hair. I always wanted little girls so I could comb, braid, and do umpteen things with their hair.

The circle of dampness grows larger and deeper into my pillow. I'm cold, but blankets hurt me. I can't bear the weight of a sheet, typical for CRPS patients. The sun has set, and the only light in the bedroom reflects in from the hallway. I can't raise myself to reach for the lamp, so I lay in the darkness until Mark comes to help me after he tucks the girls into bed.

Little feet pitter-patter back up the stairs. They run into their bedroom, and I hear Jenny climb the ladder to the bed's top bunk and picture Nicole climbing in under her purple Barney comforter on the lower bunk. The bedtime routine of songs begins, and I weep quietly so they don't hear me. I covet to also give the Barney song [5] hugs and kisses that make them giggle.

"Why am I still here, God? What's the point? I don't get to be the wife or mom I want to be or that Mark and the kids need me to be. Why don't you take me? *Please* take me, God. I will not take my life, but I'm asking you to. Please take me. I can't bear this pain another moment."

But I have dichotomous feelings and also pray, "Don't let me die, God. Please, *please* spare me so I can be with Mark and watch our kids grow. Somehow, please heal me. I want to have what we had before."

My eyes swell from the crying. I squint at my medicine bottles again. I am too in love with my family to give up. I will wake tomorrow morning and endure this nightmare all over again until either God takes me or gives me a miracle.

Mark comes in to check on me and sees my tears. He kneels on the floor beside me and strokes my hair. Looking into my eyes, he says, "I know this is hard, but we will get through this together. God will help us." We pray again for trust and healing. We have not lost hope.

HOPE

The next day our neighbor came over to help carry me down the stairs so Mark could take me to a warm water therapy pool. We went week after week, and one day, I put one foot in front of the other. My first step in two years! It felt amazing, but I could only do one. My brain had to be retrained how to walk. As I spent time in the water, I became stronger, and endorphins began firing to my brain.

I gained enough strength to sit up for five minutes, then ten, then twenty. As I sat, I read about nutrition to try to heal myself. I had enrolled in a program a few years prior and begun reading for my first class. Now I was motivated to learn nutritional remedies that could help me get better. Mark bought ingredients for a protein shake, which he began making daily for me. The amino acids were good for my brain and muscles, and I wasn't turning away these shakes like other foods. Drinking calories was easier than eating them. I managed to gain a couple of pounds—and some hope.

A FEW MONTHS LATER

While little four-year-old Nicole and I sat at the kitchen table playing with her barn animals, she said, "Mommy, you're getting better! Look!" She pointed to the muscle between my thumb and forefinger. Before it was sunken; now there was somewhat of a bulge. How on earth did she notice that little muscle? But she was right, my muscles *were* growing! At first, my smile was quivery, but after practice, my cheek muscles returned. I smiled back at my little girl as she smiled at me.

EARLY 2003

My favorite nutrition subject became amino acids because it was the protein I noticed making the most significant difference in my healing. I submitted my first test for my master's program. I was three years behind in a four-year curriculum, but my program was already making a difference in my health. Thanks to pool therapy and healthy foods, I was able to take a few steps on land now.

One morning, I hobbled from the car, over the grass, and to the side of a soccer field. I was finally able to attend a game. The parents cheered for me as if I had scored a hat trick! That night, after the kids' bath time, I hobbled again from my bed to tuck the girls into theirs. We sang the Barney song, and this time the *kids* cried. It *did* matter I was still here. God was graciously giving me back what he had given me before.

THE YEAR 2004

I got into the car, the driver's seat this time, and drove the girls to soccer practice. It was my first drive in four years. I was doing mom stuff again! Studying in the van while the kids were at soccer practice worked perfectly because it didn't take time away from "us."

When we got home, Mark and I walked holding hands down the sidewalk to the end of the block. Eventually, we made love again. It had been years. I held the girls close and cuddled with them in the recliner. My nerve pain was miraculously dissipating. I wrote papers for school about my physical, mental, emotional, and spiritual improvements. Implementing nutritional remedies and pool therapy was healing my body, mood, and spirit. Given the circumstances, my college granted an extension for my program. It took six years, but in 2007, I finally received my Master of Science degree in Holistic Nutrition.

THE YEAR 2005

My family and I moved into a house with a main-floor master bedroom for wheelchair access. I liked that our new neighbors and the parents of our kids' new friends didn't know everything about my disabled life. It was a welcomed fresh start. I began running errands, attending school functions, and going on dates with my hubby. Oh yeah, and I opened my nutrition counseling practice in 2008. I guess you could say I was my first client. And you know what? After a couple more years, I had no pain and the CRPS *completely* disappeared. This is almost unheard of! With my counselor's help, over time, I also weaned off my medications, including the hazardous opioid OxyContin my body and brain had become dependent on.

THE YEAR 2010

I practiced sports nutrition with my teen daughters, and the local high school hired me to teach sports nutrition to their athletes. My nutritional opus was an all-day event walking in heels again—demonstrating how eating healthy foods can heal the body. I taught the teen athletes how to eat to gain a competitive edge in their sport.

God gave me my miracle. Not only did he physically heal me, but he gave me back the ability to care for my family, as well as an unexpected, exciting new career.

Those years of painful torment I endured were some of the best years of my life. Yes, *best*. Not at the time, but *after* the sculpting. Best because without sculpting, I wouldn't value my current life the way I do. God's molding of me helped me understand hope comes from his goodness. If we trust in God's goodness, we can hope for good things during suffering, especially the gift of knowing him in deeper ways. He always gives us reasons to hope because he wants what is best for us. I don't know what my current life would be like had I not gone through that horrific tragedy, but I don't believe it would be as enriched. Everything is more exciting, colorful, exhilarating, precious, sensory, and alive.

TWICE

However, just because we go through tragedy once, doesn't mean we are exempt from experiencing tragedy again. I am learning I can survive my worst fears. Even twice. I have been unable to walk again for three years and counting.

I have not given up hope. I remember being grateful, in hindsight, for the ways God revealed his goodness to me during my first disability. I am learning to sit in fear and not be afraid because I know God's plans for me are always good. He showed me that before. I believe gifts in suffering are most often given in hindsight so we can grow in trust during its ravages. When I suffer, I am called to a place of discomfort, a place I do not want to be, but a place where God chooses to grow me. It's a place where I must turn around to face him so he can lead in the direction of his choosing. I am not in control. But that's a good thing!

I don't believe we can understand hope without suffering, and that's why he allows it. "Now faith is being sure of what we hope for and certain of what we do not see" (Heb. 11:1). We can be certain of God working on our behalf because he is good. We can't see how, because he works in ways we don't understand, but he meets us in our suffering, so we don't have to fear. "So do not fear, for I am with you; do not be dismayed, for I am your God. I will strengthen you and help you; I will uphold you with my righteous right hand" (Isa. 41:10).

God is here with me. Not in my imagination, but in presence. He and I are together as I struggle to understand why he would heal me, then allow me to be disabled again. I do not know whether I will ever walk more than a few steps again. Suffering in our lives often doesn't make sense, but God always has a purpose for it, always for our benefit. Jesus dying on the cross didn't make sense, but God had an immense purpose for it—the salvation of our souls. He is our ultimate hope. His plans are better than ours, so we have reason to hope even though we don't understand his allowance of our troubles. Faith is being sure of what we hope for.

The cross I am carrying, and thorns I bear, are paving the way toward receiving a heavenly crown. "Blessed is the one who perseveres under trial because, having stood the test, that person will receive the crown of life that the Lord has promised to those who love him" (James 1:12).

CHAPTER 2

The Gift of Perseverance – Keep Reaching

How can we know what perseverance is
until we've run out of strength?

HINDSIGHT

As we look at some of the healing occurrences recorded in the Bible, one striking omission stands out—the names of those Jesus healed; for instance, he refers to "the bleeding woman" and "the man with the shriveled hand." There are a few people named, like (blind) Bartimaeus, Malchus (the high priest's servant), and Lazarus. I like to think the reason most are unnamed is so we can insert our names to relate at a personal level.

Imagine you are selling your home and have decorated it for showings. Your realtor suggests taking your family photos off the walls, because if potential buyers see your family, they have a tough time imagining the home as theirs. I think the same concept applies to the healing occurrences in the Bible. They become more relatable to us without specific names attached. Jesus holds out the same kind of love, hope, and compassion for us. He knows your needs and has a healing story for you as well.

What an astounding gift of hindsight we have been given! The healing miracles were recorded for *our* benefit. "For truly I tell you, many prophets and righteous people longed to see what you see but did not see it, and to hear what you hear but did not hear it" (Matt. 13:17). We get to see what prophets did not get to see but prophesied about. The fulfillment of these prophesies provides hope for us and a framework from which to learn.

THE BLEEDING WOMAN

What we know about the woman with the issue of blood (hemorrhaging or menorrhagia—prolonged menstrual bleeding) was that she bled for twelve years (Luke 8:42–48). In the Old Testament, whenever a woman bled during her monthly cycle, she was unclean and could not be in public or go into the temple for seven days following (Lev. 15). Anything or anyone she touched would then also be unclean. Because she was supposedly contagious, she was cast from society.

For twelve years, the woman had been alone, bleeding. No one touching her; her touching no one. Ponder that for a minute, then imagine the day the bleeding woman heard Jesus was in town. She must have schemed a plan to disguise herself so her faith could get her to Jesus. He was like a magnet, and the pull on her was so powerful, *nothing* was going to stop her. As she left her dwelling, this undoubtedly feeble, desperate woman pushed through the jam-packed crowd to reach for Jesus' cloak. "If I only touch his cloak, I will be healed." If A, then B. The only "if" to the story was if she could get to his cloak.

Her faith would not let Jesus get away. The woman's plan was to touch his cloak unnoticed—but Jesus notices exceptional faith. As he felt power flow out of him, she felt her blood flow stop. Jesus stopped, turned around, and looked for who touched him. The woman, realizing she was found out, came and fell trembling at his feet, telling him the truth. She had to tell him she was unclean. But it was okay. He was the atoning sacrifice for her sin and the healer of her condition. He affirmed her faith, saying to her, "Daughter, your faith has healed you. Go in peace and be freed from your suffering" (Mark 5:34). She received gifts of healing and peace. "Peace I leave with you; my peace I give you. I do not give to you as the world gives. Do not let your hearts be troubled and do not be afraid" (John 14:27).

The bleeding woman's faith moved Jesus to action, even though he was on his way to heal the synagogue ruler's dying daughter. It seems fitting her story is sandwiched within the synagogue ruler's so he could witness her healing and welcome her back to the synagogue.

What do you think the bleeding woman felt when Jesus called her "daughter?" She had been adopted into his family. She now belonged somewhere—to someone. Her faith taught the community surrounding her that the Old Testament teachings on blood issues were just that. Old. Old laws. The revolutionary Jesus was in town leading a revolutionary way—those previously considered on top of the religious hierarchy are bump, bump, bumped to the bottom, and those who mourn, the meek, poor in spirit, pure in heart, and those persecuted are now considered great in the kingdom of God (Matt. 5:3–12).

Jesus considered stigmatized outcasts integral to society, so he wove them back in where they belonged. He taught, "When you give a luncheon or dinner, do not invite your friends, your brothers or sisters, your relatives, or your rich neighbors; if you do, they may invite you back and so you will be repaid. But when you give a banquet, invite the poor, the crippled, the lame, the blind, and you will be blessed. Although they cannot repay you, you will be repaid at the resurrection of the righteous" (Luke 14:12–14).

All are welcome to approach Jesus. He excludes no one. As Nancy Guthrie says, "Would you take comfort and find confidence in knowing that although the purpose in your suffering may be unseen, God does have a purpose, and part of that purpose is to display his work in your life?"[6] Suffering gives meaning to everything because it provides context. Who do you think was most excited and grateful to attend synagogue on the next Sabbath?

> ... but we also glory in our sufferings, because we know that suffering produces perseverance; perseverance, character; and character, hope. And hope does not put us to shame, because God's love has been poured out into our hearts through the Holy Spirit, who has been given to us (Rom. 5:3–5).

Guthrie further states, "Rather than running from or resenting your suffering, would you be willing to look for God in it ... God wants to use the difficulties in your life not to punish you or hurt you but to draw you to himself. Will you come?"[7] Perseverance is gifted to us from God when we feel we can't go on. Go to him as the bleeding woman did—and let nothing stop you. Let us persevere with faith until God crowns us with the crown of life in heaven. "Let perseverance finish its work so that you may be mature and complete, not lacking anything" (James 1:4).

There is a "crown of life" in heaven designated for those who have persevered under trial. It is available to you and me. The bleeding woman is wearing a crown because of her immense suffering and faithful perseverance. As I type, I cry because daily perseverance through chronic pain is really, really hard, but her story gives me hope. I have a feeling we will be wonderful friends in heaven one day. After all, she is the one who inspired the writing of this book. She's the one who persevered and touched the fringe of Jesus' cloak, but even more, she touched his heart.

CHAPTER 3

The Gift of Compassion – Unexpected Blessings

How can we know what compassion is until we've
emulated it to the degree Jesus exemplified it?

THE INVALID

When Jesus was in Jerusalem for a feast, he saw and approached an invalid lying by the Sheep Gate pool. Unlike the story of the bleeding woman, John 5:2–15 tells us that Jesus took the initiative and learned the man had been disabled for thirty-eight years. That's longer than Jesus had been alive! Jesus asked him, "Do you want to get well?" It seems like a question that requires a simple yes or no answer, but the man replied, "Sir, I have no one to help me into the pool when the water is stirred. While I am trying to get in, someone else goes down ahead of me."

Could his answer possibly be an excuse? Was he avoiding responsibility? Why didn't he just answer the question with a "yes" if he wanted to get well? Had he given up? Was he indifferent, apathetic, comfortable, or lazy? To me, he seems stuck, lying around the pool for thirty-eight long years.

The invalid does not seem to have faith—he doesn't even know who Jesus is. But Jesus wasn't reliant on a person's expression of faith to heal them. He healed people who had faith, and he healed those with no faith. Jesus' heartfelt compassion reached out and instantly healed the man, who was then instructed to pick up his mat and walk. Of course, the Jews pointed out that he should not be carrying his mat on the Sabbath, according to the law.

Jesus was more concerned about man than the law, but the Pharisees (religious leaders) were more concerned about the law than man. They didn't rejoice with the invalid that he was walking. They didn't acknowledge the healing at all! Instead, they wanted to find the "lawbreaking" man who cured a man that could not walk for thirty-eight years. But Jesus had slipped away into the crowd.

Later, when they learned it was Jesus who healed someone *again* on the Sabbath, the Pharisees persecuted him and began trying to kill him. Someone should have reminded them of the sixth commandment of the law of Moses, "You shall not murder" (Ex. 20:13).

THE EFFECTS OF SIN ON PHYSIOLOGY

Sometimes, our diseases and disabilities can be caused by sin. Not necessarily, and not always, but sometimes. John doesn't describe the reason the man was disabled, but when Jesus later found him, and they spoke again, Jesus implied the man's sin at least contributed to his illness. He said, "See, you are well again. Stop sinning, or something worse may happen to you" (John 5:14). Jesus gave a blessing to the bleeding woman, "go in peace," but to the invalid he gave a warning, "stop sinning ...."

The biblical notation on this verse in the 2008 NIV Study Bible says:

Stop sinning implies that the man's sins had caused his disability. In John 9:1 [about a man born blind], he repudiates the idea that disabilities (such as blindness) are inevitably caused by sin, but he does not say they are never caused by sin. "Something worse" means the eternal consequences of sin are more serious than any physical ailment.[8]

No one likes to think that their physical disability or ailment is due to sin. This is difficult for anyone to accept. But it does not mean it is not valid, even in part, for some people. For example, the overconsumption of alcohol over time causes liver disease. Whatever sin the invalid was committing, he was told by Jesus to walk away from it, or something worse might happen.

Compassion drove Jesus to heal the invalid. Whatever the reason for the man's disability didn't matter to Jesus, as long as he repented of his sin. Jesus didn't judge him, then walk away. He cared for him as much as he cared for those with extraordinary faith. Sometimes our faith catches Jesus' attention, and sometimes we are beneficiaries of his compassion. Nothing we do can make God stop caring about us.

THE YEAR 2002

When you stare death in the face, you need many things, counseling being one of them. Thankfully, my counselor sat by my bedside weekly. For four months, Christina tried to talk me into getting a wheelchair and a stair glide so I could participate in life outside of my prison cell bedroom. My stubborn pride kept me confined. "I'll be better soon; I don't need those things," was my sincere excuse. But after I kept not getting better, I finally grasped the fact that I had to learn to live as a disabled person, so with a grumbling heart, I asked my doctor for a prescription for both.

With Halloween approaching, Christina confronted my prideful disposition, "You have a choice. Either you stay home by yourself, or you get up and go trick-or-treating in the wheelchair with your family." But I didn't want my neighbors to see me in this condition. I was only 35. No one else I knew had to live life from a wheelchair. I realized then that I was still imprisoned. Although my prison cell expanded to the size of our home (thanks to the stair glide), I didn't feel free to be me around other people. I was utterly embarrassed, but my embarrassment was keeping me from getting well, so I chose to trick-or-treat. I was seeing how I was like the invalid lying by the pool for thirty-eight years. I was holding myself back from getting better by making excuses. My pride didn't want me to get a wheelchair. My insecurity didn't want me to have relationships. Like the invalid, I needed to repent. My pride and insecurity were hindering my physical, emotional, mental, and spiritual improvement.

For the next two years, I lived from that wheelchair, participating in family life. The kids loved to push me around. And if you've never owned a stair glide, get one if you want to have the coolest house on the block. Neighborhood kids came over frequently for a ride. My other "ride," the wheelchair, gave me bonus points with the kids. Then, when we put a bed in our living room, oh my goodness, we could have made a few bucks had we charged an entrance fee for those little monkeys jumpin' on the bed!

The kids didn't see my disability; they saw *me* and thought my assistive devices were pretty cool toys. Their acceptance of me gave me courage to trust adults again, and my "toys" eventually helped God lead me to my recovery. My assistive devices helped free me, not confine or define me. God, in his compassion, healed me like he did the man who couldn't walk for thirty-eight years. I too had to repent of sins confining me.

COMPASSION AND ACCEPTANCE

One day, while our Jenny was in third grade, we received a call from the school telling us she had forgotten her lunch. Mark found it by the front door and ran it over to the school. From the parking lot, he saw the children out at recess and spotted our Jennifer Joy. She was on the blacktop, spinning a boy around in his wheelchair, playing with him during recess. Jen was not put off by people in wheelchairs; her mom used one. This boy, who other kids marginalized because of his disability, was compassionately and lovingly cared for by our Jenny. We learned later from her teachers that it was a regular occurrence for Jen to spend her lunch and recess with this disabled boy. How did she learn to have that kind of compassion? From God, who allowed her to grow up with a disabled mom.

Jen is now a graduate student studying to become a child life specialist, a liaison between the doctor and the child and family to help make hospital stays and medical procedures less scary for children. Jennifer is one of the most compassionate people on the face of the earth. If you know her, you are nodding your head in agreement.

Our Nicole, two-and-a-half years younger than Jen, is also in graduate school, researching how children develop the concept of pain. She has also been a recipient of God's gift of embodying compassion. She grew up with a mother in pain and still watches me cry out in anguish and struggle to walk. Is it any wonder she wants to understand pain and research how to make a difference in the lives of us who experience it? Nicole is the most nonjudgmental person I know. She is accepting of everyone and convicts me during my critical moments.

During this crisis, I worried how my disability would affect our children, but as time goes on, it becomes more apparent that God, in his wisdom, knew what he was allowing and how to teach his/our children to be more like him through suffering. When we suffer, we are carved, and it hurts. God chisels us through anguish to fulfill the ultimate purpose he has for our lives and even for those around us. Love includes pain because love is the chisel that forms us into who he designed us to be. I prayed for our kids to embody compassion, and they are embracing it beautifully. They are benefactors of love that was wrapped up in the guise of pain.

This is just one example of how God formed their characters

during a rough few years of their young lives. If only I had hindsight when I worried for them. Or rather, if only I had trusted God that he was working his plan for the good of all of us during severe hardship. Mark and I could *not* have taught our girls to embody the depth of compassion they developed during those tough years and still carry with them into adulthood. What beautiful gifts *God* has given his/our children.

CHAPTER 4

The Gift of Deliverance – Not Through Man's Ingenuity

How can we know what it means to be delivered until we've surrendered?

DISABILITY TAKE TWO

Mark walked Jen down the aisle, but I couldn't see them very well from the front row. However, I had a clear view of Stephen trying to hold it together. He was crying, overflowing with love while watching his almost bride step closer to him at each beat of the music. His face during those moments solidified my belief that he and Jen chose well. When Mark and Jen reached the front row, she held out her hand for mine, and I stepped into the aisle. I held her hand while Mark and I stood on either side of our oldest daughter and answered, "we do," in unison to the question, "Who gives this woman to be married to this man?" And we gave our daughter to join her life with Stephen's.

Dinner, cake, dancing, and glow sticks followed, and then they were off, and the cleaning crew got on it. As I walked by a stack of heavy wooden chairs leaning against the wall, one of them slid down and attacked my ankle with force. I knew at that moment my life was changed for a long time to come. The chair re-triggered the Complex Regional Pain Syndrome in my body and initiated another fight for my life.

It's freaky and frustrating how many things in life I have to do twice (usually computer stuff). It should have been a simple sprained ankle, but the overcompensated foot is still trying to bear weight. I have struggled in my faith throughout this trial. I have questioned God: "Why this *again?*" In my lowest moments I felt like God didn't care about me. I just could not see deliverance. For a time, I stopped praying.

SURRENDER FOR DELIVERANCE

I'm not the only one who has felt God didn't care about them. In Exodus 14, Moses led the Israelites out of Egypt after 400 years of bondage. One problem: Moses led them to the Red Sea. Some leader. No one even knew to bring a swimming suit. But all this time, God was telling Moses precisely what to do, and Moses trusted him even though circumstances looked grim. Moses told the people not to be afraid, to stand firm, and watch the deliverance the Lord was about to bring. He continued, "The LORD will fight for you; you need only to be still" (Ex.14:13–14). The Red Sea lay ahead, the Egyptians approached from behind, and the Israelites were supposed to be still? That goes against all instincts for survival! But God does this kind of thing to help us understand it's not the ingenuity of man that delivers us, it's God.

Then there's a curious next verse when God tells Moses to stop praying. Have you ever heard of such a thing? Me neither, until I discovered it this morning. Moses must have said a silent prayer crying out to God, but it's not recorded in the Bible—just alluded to. "Then the LORD said to Moses, 'Why are you crying out to me? Tell the Israelites to move on. Raise your staff and stretch out your hand over the sea to divide the water so that the Israelites can go through the sea on dry ground'" (Ex. 14:15–16).

After Moses told the people to be still and trust God, then God said move. There is a time to be still, and then God tells us when to move. God basically said to Moses and the people, "You prayed for deliverance, so here we go!" He parts the sea, and they get going.

TAKE ACTION

I found a similar story in Joshua, where Joshua had just "[torn] his clothes and [fallen] facedown before the ark of the LORD, remaining there till evening" (Josh. 7:6-13). Joshua was lamenting in prayer, and the LORD told him to stand up and go. Take action! God heard his prayer, and now it was time to do something about it. God told Joshua he wouldn't deliver his people until they repented and got rid of the things they had stolen. God *wanted* to deliver them, but their sins were preventing him from doing so.

Prayer, repentance, and obedience work together. God uses the people who pray prayers to answer those very prayers. When I removed myself from prayer, I removed myself from intimacy with God and from his deliverance. God allowed me to be injured after the wedding, and I just sat down at my Red Sea/Jordan River and languished. I could not see how God could deliver me from this pain. After I finally got up off my face, I prayed for deliverance, and God used this pain in my life to help heal different pains.

- A judgmental thought righted
- A grudge forgiven
- A person taken for granted now prioritized
- A vicissitude accepted
- A greed freed
- An ingratitude turned grateful
- A hypocritical thought humbled
- A self-demeaning thought extinguished
- An evil thought destroyed
- An envy rectified
- A ruminating thought redirected
- A strength beyond self sought
- A panicked heart stilled
- A perspective changed

One injury is healing many others. God works in mysterious ways.

CHAPTER 5

The Gift of Love – Better Than a Hallmark Love

*How can we know what love is without allowing
ourselves to receive it?*

BETTER THAN A HALLMARK LOVE

When Mark and I first met in the late 1980s, he was kind of interested in someone else, so I made him a cheesecake. Turns out, it was a good idea to spend the $3.99 on that boxed confection. Yes, some cheesy cheesecakes come in boxes, but that turned his affections toward me. Before we went on our first date, we had a predate when we were on dates with (not dating) other people. I know, let me explain.

The occasion was a Moroccan-themed dinner with twelve couples. As we entered the dining area, we feasted our eyes on the vibrant colors of the décor. Floor pillows surrounded several coffee tables where we ate our Moroccan meals. My date was a co-worker, and we went to this party as friends. Mark was invited by a friend as well. It just so happened that my friend-date and Mark's friend-date were two of the chefs preparing this extravagant meal. My assigned table for four, minus two chefs, left this guy named Mark and me to fend for ourselves. We talked throughout dinner, as various chefs brought us more delectable meats and vegetables to try. By the time we were ready to watch *Casa Blanca*, I wasn't thinking about couscous or Morocco; my mind and heart were thinking about Marko!

The following week, when Mark called to ask me out on our first official date, my heart flitted with excitement. What a telephone voice! He sounded so mature, so handsome (Hallmarkish)! A year and a half later, we tied the knot.

One sentence to summarize Mark is this: he prioritizes his loves. God comes first, me second, our daughters third, and work fourth. Augustine, in his book, *On Christian Doctrine,* expounds on this concept:

> But living a just and holy life requires one to be capable of an objective and impartial evaluation of things: to love things, that is to say, in the right order, so that you do not love what is not to be loved, or fail to love what is to be loved, or have a greater love for what should be loved less, or an equal love for things that should be loved less or more, or a lesser or greater love for things that should be loved equally.[9]

When Mark looked into my eyes on our wedding day and said, "I will always be faithful to you" and "I will love you in sickness and in health," they were words that, as the years rolled by, would become even more loving and meaningful to me. Mark has done both, despite the severe challenges we have faced with my physical pain.

One of the most challenging times in our marriage was when I was bedridden. The CRPS made me so sensitive to touch that I could not hold or be held by Mark. My nerves over-fired, and any slight touch to my skin sent me over the moon in pain. For years, I couldn't bake Mark a boxed cheesecake, take him on a date, physically express my love for him, greet him at the door, or walk side-by-side holding hands. At times, I wondered why he stuck around.

We didn't know if I'd get better, if I were going to die, or if I'd be rendered permanently unable to walk. But Mark's loves were prioritized. He loved God more than me. By loving God more than me, he followed God's command to love his wife as he cares for himself (Eph. 5:28–33). In his mind, it has never been an option to leave me, even though it was a legitimate fear of mine.

When you are the recipient of the kind of love that keeps giving, and you can't give much back, it deepens your understanding and appreciation of love. Love should have no strings attached. It gives without expectation of receiving anything back. God has been teaching me how to receive love. For some of us, it's harder than you might think.

Recently, Mark and I have found ourselves in a remarkably similar place. I am not bedridden, but I can't walk again. Mark has stood by me, and I am more secure than ever in his love because his priorities have been demonstrated and maintained throughout our thirty years of marriage. He spends time with God every day before I get up, and he closes his day in prayer with me and then alone with God.

Jesus was the prime example of loving his Father first, and the Bible teaches us this is the way to love.

As the Father has loved me, so have I loved you. Now remain in my love. If you obey my commands, you will remain in my love, just as I have obeyed my Father's commands and remain in his love. I have told you this so that my joy may be in you and that your joy may be complete. My command is this: Love each other as I have loved you. Greater love has no one than this, that he lay down his life for his friends (John 15:9–13).

Mark lays his life down for me every day.

From October 2018 through February 2019, I could use neither my hands nor feet because of mind-blowing nerve and orthopedic pain. I had hurt my hands by trying to compensate for my feet. Later, I wrote in my journal:

Mark moves me from place to place and moves furniture to accommodate my needs. He pulls up a mattress from the basement and places it in the middle of our living room, so I don't have to be in the bedroom all day. He moves the commode from here to there, helping me on and off, then emptying, cleansing, and sanitizing it. He removes my insecurities and embarrassment. He dries my tears, looking into my eyes, and recommits his love for me. He moves my heart.

Mark bathes and dresses me, detangles, brushes, and dries my hair. He calms me by reading to me or finding soothing music to play on my tablet. He lies gently beside me, being careful not to intensify my pain, but he wants to look into my eyes and be beside me. He assures me he will always be by my side. He dries our tears and tenderly kisses my forehead. We memorize a Bible verse, then pray. Sometimes we sing. Whatever helps me get through a few more minutes.

Every weekday he takes me, in my wheelchair, to various doctors' appointments and unsuccessful therapy pool visits, helping me through the meticulous and painful effort to get there, and then consoles me through the disappointment and resulting breakdowns. He picks up my prescriptions and follows my tedious medicinal and supplemental schedules. He buys a gazillion dollars' worth of worthless insoles, medical supplies, medicine, and no diagnosis.

Mark shops for the food and cooks all the meals. To lighten my heart's heaviness, Mark often uses food art to decorate my turkey burgers with smiley faces made with ketchup, mushrooms, and pickles. He places me ahead of his job and says, "You come first."

He comforts our adult daughters, extending words of encouragement. Mark anticipates my needs by buying a new puzzle to build together to help my fingers regain functionality. Weekly, he brings me fresh flowers. "It's bringing the outdoors inside to be with you." I'm not kidding about the weekly.

We pray for sleep and peace. It's my only break from pain and a rare reprieve for him from our predicament.

Currently, I'm not as dependent on Mark. We are relentlessly tested and know full well we aren't beyond Satan's schemes to break us apart. Sometimes we fight and give each other the silent treatment then search the house for chocolate. We've both broken down in tears, not understanding one another's perspective. There are times we just don't get each other; nothing said is taken right, or everything said is taken wrong. It has been difficult to be in this season of hardship, but God has allowed this trial in our marriage to strengthen us ultimately. We can't know all the reasons, but we trust they are for our good (Jer. 29:11–14).

Overall, in our marriage, Mark reflects Jesus to me, providing a glimpse into what heaven will be like. I feel so loved, cared for, and amazed by his dedication to me. I have a clearer picture of who Jesus is because of his kindness. He has helped me understand my relationship with God more than anyone. I look into his eyes and down into his soul, and I see the closest thing to heaven I have experienced. Sometimes it makes me cry.

However, Mark is not Jesus.

Jesus is *even more* loving and faithful to me. He will also dry my tears one day and take away all my pain (Rev. 21:4). He is my ultimate Healer. He will give me eternal life to relish in our love forever. This better-than-a-Hallmark love story is about the Jesus of the Bible, who traded in his crown of thorns to offer us not a small finger ring of gold and diamonds, but instead a heavenly eternal crown. He holds out his proposal to us every day, whether married, single, widowed, or divorced. He wants to be with us for eternity. There has never been, nor ever will be, anyone who loves us more. He invites us to feast with him at his dinner table for eternity if we accept his proposal with a "Yes, of course, I will!" response.

Whatever God allows in your life may not play out like the stories on the Hallmark Channel, but you can experience the best love of your life if you trust in him. He has a plan for you. He has healing waiting for you. The Bible says God has set eternity in our hearts so that one day we might seek and find him. He made us to want to be in a relationship with him (Ecc. 3:11).

This kind of love story is better than a Hallmark love because the characters are not fictional. The love story of Jesus holds the purest selfless love we can ever find. He is fiercely in love with you and with me. "Yes, of course, I will!" I said to Mark in June 1991 to a marriage on this side of heaven, but even before that proposal, I told Jesus on July 5, 1985, "Yes, of course, I will!" in response to his proposal for an eternal marriage.

CHAPTER 6

The Gift of Grace – Divine Intervention

*How can we understand grace until we've realized our
profound need for forgiveness?*

DUST

In 1991, six weeks after our engagement, Mark and I moved to
Los Angeles from Denver. We were asked to help with a church
plant there. We decided our wedding would be in California—
the place where we'd begin our married life together. Mom and
Dad provided the money for our wedding expenses: enough to
rent a church, our pastor, and Dad's tux, as well as buy a cake,
punch, and M&M's. No band, no dancing, no alcohol, no lunch,
no favors.

Our families came, but it was a financial burden on them.
Mom and Dad almost didn't make the rehearsal dinner because of
a canceled flight due to a December snowstorm and had to spend
the night at the airport. When they finally arrived, Mom looked
ghostly, ragged, and panicked. She thought she might miss her
daughter's wedding.

It was then, in horror, I realized I didn't involve Mom in my
wedding planning—a dream of every daughter's mother. Our
abrupt move to L.A. and excluding her from wedding planning
must have broken her heart. I'm sure if we got married in Den-

ver, Mom would have created centerpieces, and we certainly would have gone to get our nails done. The only way I involved Mom in our wedding was to have her light the unity candle. Wow. The rest of the time, she sat collecting dust.

Four years later, when I was pregnant, we moved back to Denver because the California housing market was financially ludicrous. We could have stayed in our one-bedroom apartment, but we didn't want our kids growing up playing in the alley with trash can lids and mangy dogs.

REROUTING

Our girls were six and eight when we took a trip with Mom to Durango. She had wanted us to go for years. The day after we arrived, I looked at the large bruise on her leg. "Mom, you didn't have that before hanging up the laundry." She had just come back inside the cabin and looked down at her purplish thigh.

"Oh, I'm sure it's nothing, honey." But it was. I knew it was. People don't bruise that easily from simply resting a load of laundry on their leg. Mom was not one to draw attention to herself. She was concerned regularly for her kids and grandkids but brushed her issues off as if they were dust.

Not long after our mountain vacation, I invited Mom to tour a Parade of Homes in a development filled with rolling hills near to my home. My 70-year-old, typically peppy mom needed to stop often to catch her breath. We left the unaffordable housing development and headed toward mine. Mom checked her phone messages on the way. Thirteen. We hadn't bothered with our phones the entire day. Mom became eerily somber as she listened to the hospital staff, the doctor, and Dad telling her to get to the emergency room immediately. She desperately needed blood and platelet transfusions.

Rerouting, we drove to the hospital, silence accompanying us. I held her hand, but mine needed holding too.

Aplastic anemia is a rare blood condition. She would need blood and platelet transfusions regularly. One day Mom tried to be surprisingly vulnerable with me. "I'm afraid to die." The problem-solver in me took her to get a recliner to help her sleep better. Oh, how I wish I had just sat and listened to her instead.

Two years later, Mom was still getting occasional transfusions. She came over for an evening to hang with the kids and spent the night with us. On the morning of July 17, 2007, I hugged her before she stepped into her black Dodge Durango. Then she was off. I stood in the driveway waving goodbye until she was out of sight.

DURANGO

The state patrol met my dad and siblings at the crash site a few weeks later. Warmed by the sun, we think Mom fell asleep at the wheel during her six-hour drive to Durango. She hadn't slept very well in her recliner the night before or the night before that, but wanted to go anyway. She was taking her 16-year-old granddaughter Christina for a getaway to her mountain cabin.

The mile marker on the side of the road was mangled and bent almost to the ground. Skid marks were deep and black, long and winding across the four-lane highway and off to the opposite side of the road. The vehicle rolled four times, pinning her. Sixteen-year-old Christina climbed out of a broken window and onto shattered glass and fire ants, shoeless. Flight For Life revived Mom on the way to the hospital, but she was in terrible shape. The family met at the hospital to say goodbye to our unconscious Mom, who looked, well, not much like Mom. Our little eight-year-old Nicole wailed in anguish for her grandma, and the hospital staff felt the collective expression of our pain and wept with us.

However, at another hospital lay my niece, who was granted grace in the form of a saved life. Mom's car was completely mangled, except where Christina sat. It seemed God cupped Christina in his hands as the car tumbled. It was not her time to go. He still had magnificent plans for her life.

THE CRASH SITE

Shattered glass and fractured car parts remained at the crash site. The state patrol said he had gathered all the belongings that tumbled out of the car so we wouldn't find anything of value there. Nevertheless, we paced the roadside dirt hoping to find traces of what once belonged to Mom. I looked to the sky asking God for a sign that she was okay.

And then I found it—part of an earring glinting beneath the dirt. Game on. Nearby, one of my siblings found another earring. Then her ladybug pair. Then one of her Native American storyteller earrings—her favorite. Remnants of Mom. The treasure hunt continued until we found several matching pairs of Mom's earrings, including the match to her storyteller pair. These I would clean and give to Dad. What an unexpected gift. What a sudden and unexpected end to life. Mom was only 72. Her dad had lived to 105, so we expected she would follow suit. But we were so painfully wrong.

I laid on the closet floor looking at family photos, rolling back and forth in the fetal position. "I still want you!" I screamed and cried. "I still need you!" Years later, I continued rolling on the floor, yelling, "I still want you, Mom!" I couldn't heal. I didn't say goodbye. I told her I'd call her before she left on her trip, but I didn't. I was too wrapped up in my nutrition studies. Mom was afraid to die, and I was not there for her in a way she tried to ask me to be. Because of this, I was clothed in guilt and pushed grace away. I didn't deserve forgiveness; she was my mom. I wanted to redo adulthood to prioritize her, so she felt valued, but I had had my chance; it was too late.

After Mom died, we learned aplastic anemia is fatal without a bone marrow transplant, which she was denied because of her age. Why didn't we know this? Why didn't Mom tell us? She knew she was dying, and she tried to talk about it. When she said, "I'm afraid to die," I didn't know she *really was* dying. Mom didn't press the issue because she brushed her issues off as dust. Regretfully, I did too.

DREAMS

God has communicated through dreams since the beginning of time. For instance, God gave a promise to Jacob,[10] a discerning heart to Solomon,[11] revealed the future to Joseph,[12] directed Jacob and his family to go to Egypt to be with Joseph,[13] and warned the Magi[14] through dream appearances. The Bible describes around two hundred occasions where God intervened through dreams.[15] And he worked through dreams to heal my broken heart.

I prayed for four years for my heart to heal from my profound grief over my mother's sudden death. Then one night I had a dream about her—then another, then another. At first, Mom was distant, facing the opposite direction. Then slowly, each night, we drew closer together.

THE YEAR 2011

- She was off in the distance, her back turned to me. I called out, "Mom! Mom!" I knew it was her and ran as fast as I could, but I couldn't reach her, and she couldn't hear me.
- Her short blonde hair looked beautiful from behind. I was closer this time; despite that, she couldn't hear me. Why wasn't she responding? Didn't she miss me too?
- I could see her face! Why did she turn around and walk the other way? She obviously hadn't seen me, or she would have run to me. Surely, she would have run to me, right?

- I talked to her, but she wouldn't talk back. I was close enough to see the beauty of her Norwegian blue eyes.
- I had to run into the bathroom during the event. Was it ever busy in there! So busy, I ran right smack into the lady with a long tan coat and fluffy baby blue scarf. I looked up at her to apologize, and it was Mom. I grabbed on to as much of her as I could to keep her in my grasp. I sobbed and hugged. She cried too and held on to me with all her might: tears, but no words. I woke up, still feeling her embrace.
- When Mom began speaking, we were in my car going on a drive, talking, and laughing. Mom's royal blue blouse was so vivid. She was within reach in the passenger seat. It was like a normal day together.
- Mom and Dad, along with my siblings, were at a family reunion. The usual activities took place—singing, s'mores, swimming, playing Wild Whist. Our entire family was together again.

And then the dreams stopped.

I had the chance to make fresh memories with Mom. Before I went to sleep, Mark would say, "Enjoy your time with your mom!" I believe it was the grace of God helping one of his grieving daughters get unstuck. Mom appearing to me in my dreams nightly for over a month could not be coincidental.

Harold Kushner, in his book, *When Bad Things Happen to Good People* wisely states, "When miracles occur ... we would be well advised to bow our heads in thanks at the presence of a miracle, and not think that our prayers, contributions, or abstentions are what did it. The next time we try, we may wonder why our prayers are ineffective."[16] A divine gift of grace was given to me, not earned. Suffering has confirmed for me there is a God, for miracles can only come from him. He has healed pains and solved problems no other being, or icon, could solve.

After spending time with Mom in my dreams, my heart finally healed. I felt closure. I have not laid on the floor screaming out in emotional pain since. I can listen to Christmas music again and enjoy hearing her voice sing along in my mind. And, finally, I weaned off my antidepressant.

I will see Mom again one day, but until then, I don't have to leave my life behind with hers on the day she died. I still have purpose and people to love. I'm thankful for the healing that happens on earth. God still heals through dreams and in other mysterious ways.

One of the Hebrew names for God is Jehovah Rapha, "the God who heals." The word "Rapha" translates to "to make whole completely, to mend and repair thoroughly."[17]

He heals the brokenhearted
  and binds up their wounds (Ps. 147:3).

Jesus clothed me in his grace, a gift I had no words for. That's how grace works.

CHAPTER 7

The Gift of Courage – He Didn't Run Away

*How can we know what courage is until
we do something beyond our capabilities?*

THE MAN WITH THE SHRIVELED HAND

In Jesus' day, the religious leaders were all about keeping legalistic rules and shunned those who did not follow them. Jesus sliced through their religious arrogance with his words and showed them that *love* rules.

Another time Jesus went into the synagogue, and a man with a shriveled hand was there. Some of them [the Pharisees] were looking for a reason to accuse Jesus, so they watched him closely to see if he would heal him on the Sabbath. Jesus said to the man with the shriveled hand, "Stand up in front of everyone." Then Jesus asked them, "Which is lawful on the Sabbath: to do good or to do evil, to save life or to kill?" But they remained silent. He looked around at them in anger and, deeply distressed at their stubborn hearts, said to the man, "Stretch out your hand." He stretched it out, and his hand was completely restored. Then the Pharisees went out and began to plot with the Herodians how they might kill Jesus (Mark 3:1–6).

One reason Jesus used his God-given power to heal people's ailments during his earthly ministry was to establish that he was the Son of God (John 4:48). The Pharisees could not heal, the Sadducees could not heal, and the sorcerers could not heal. Only Jesus, and the Holy Spirit through men he empowered, could perform miracles, including healings (Matt. 10:1).

Three of the four Gospel writers, including Luke, a doctor, recorded the biblical story of the healing of the man with the shriveled hand.[18] Step into this man's sandals to see what he may have experienced that day. Then step back into your shoes to see how Jesus wants to provide similar healing for you. Jesus asked the man with the shriveled hand—in the synagogue, on the Sabbath—to stand in front of everyone for all to see this healing, so there would be no question of its miraculousness.

No doubt this man was in the habit of hiding his hand inside his cloak from embarrassment. Now Jesus commanded him to stand in front of everyone and stretch out his hand. The man found the courage to obey instead of running away, received healing, and inspired others in doing so.

Through bravery, if we too hold out our imperfections and weaknesses toward God, he can work his healing in our hearts and perhaps even in our physical bodies. If instead we go into hiding, others cannot see God working gloriously through our limitations. God may not choose to heal our physical imperfections during our earthly life, but our hearts can heal, and we can move closer to God the souls of many who are watching us. Like this man, we must courageously choose to obey God and not run away, even when we are afraid. We must have courage to face where we have never been.

Jesus publicly validated this man's worth and proved his point to the Pharisees and all who stood watching—that man is more valuable than rulebooks. Jesus asked the Pharisees a question, "If any of you has a sheep and it falls into a pit on the Sabbath, will you not take hold of it and lift it out? How much more valuable is a person than a sheep! Therefore it is lawful to do good on the Sabbath" (Matt. 12:11–12).

Even though Jesus knew this Sabbath healing would anger the Pharisees and initiate a conspiracy to kill him, he validated the man with the shriveled hand anyway. I am willing to bet the man stood a little taller and more confidently as Jesus endorsed his worth in front of the entire crowd, including the highly respected lawmakers. God not only healed his hand, but his emotional suffering as well.

Jesus validated the worth of all humanity that day. He made his point that following strict Pharisaical laws would no longer dictate our value. He changed law into love, spinning the direction of our future. Soon after healing this man physically, Jesus died for his spiritual healing. Jesus died for everyone's spiritual healing in that crowd, and he died to forgive and spiritually heal you and me. We are beneficiaries of the gifts his love bestows if we courageously follow and love him in return (Matt. 5:3–12).

Jesus had a perfect plan for this imperfect man to have a profound impact on the world. Now was his moment, the day he longed for, his time for physical restoration! His suffering was finally ending. The living God healed the man with the shriveled hand, who struggled to find his worth. His story fills us with the hope of restoration and being used by God. God has a plan for us too, and it is perfect, even if it involves pain.

Pain and imperfections in our lives do not equal a lack of love from God. Instead, they reveal, at the right time, a divine and perfect purpose packed with love. Hold out your hand—your fear, pain, and shortcomings—to him with courage and see what he has for you. He loves you. He died to know you.

So do not fear, for I am with you; do not be dismayed, for I am your God. I will strengthen you and help you; I will uphold you with my righteous right hand (Isa. 41:10).

I'M STILL ME

One afternoon, while I was sitting in our garage trying to get some sun, I came to the realization that my former life, as I knew it, had ended. No more running errands, no more daily walks for exercise, no more freedom to drive, and how was I going to continue to take care of Dad?

My life is different now, and I am often avoided and looked at and treated as weak. And I was, and am, but at the same time, I'm not. I'm stronger now—more courageous. I am stronger now in many ways than when I could walk. Suffering has taught me not to look at those who are obviously suffering with woeful eyes, but instead to look at them with the utmost respect. Through suffering, I have learned how to identify those who have also deeply suffered—they befriend you instead of looking away.

Relating to a sufferer is not that difficult. What makes it difficult is when your go-to question is, "How are you feeling?" There is more to us than our pain. We delight in more thoughtful and stimulating questions such as, "What have you been learning lately?" Listen carefully, you might learn something.

ABIDING DAY BY DAY

Even though I wake up every morning in pain, I say good morning to my Maker and ask him to use me somehow. I slide to the edge of the bed, breathe deeply, and pray for courage to begin my day. I have examples of courageous people set before me: people who have suffered more deeply than I have. I share some of their stories in later chapters. Their faith entices me closer to the finish line. Like C. S. Lewis says, "Aim at Heaven, and you will get earth thrown in. Aim at earth and you will get neither."[19] My friends' minds are set on the hope of heaven, and they each see their suffering as a way to glorify God.

Andrew Murray, in his book *Abiding in Christ*, writes, "Each day of faithfulness brings a blessing for the next, making both the trust and the surrender easier and more blessed. And so the Christian life grows; as we give our whole heart to the work of each day. And so each day separately, all the day continually, and day by day successively, we abide in Jesus."[20]

I want my life to provide hope and courage for others. I don't want to be pitied. I want people to know I'm still me despite my limitations—I'm still what lies inside of me. I think that's how the man with the shriveled hand felt. He wanted to be known for who he was on the inside and not be defined by his disability. I want to have courage as he did, to hold out my disability to God for him to use in the way of his choosing. God will be with me wherever I go. I need only to be strong and courageous.

Courage

Tears untamed
Mascara-stained face
Like black rivers
Flow incessantly.
Sculpting new features:
Furrowed brow,
Eyes scowl,

Dimples disappear.
Lips pursed,
Smiles cursed,
All so well-rehearsed.

Pain asunder
Pulls me under
'neath the former
Life I've lost.

Time escaping,
Memories fading
Of the former
Life I've lost.

Still I live.
Still,
I live.
I am still
Imprisoned in this body
Drowning in
Unfathomable pain
Looming darkness
Sinister doubt
And inflexible fear.

Yet

Beneath black rivers
Tears run clear
To my soul
Arousing tender shoots.

Tears untamed
Clear the way
For new life to begin.
What's grieved has passed,
The die is cast.

Courage sought,
Brows part
Lifting eyes to see.
I am still
All that lies within.
Strength rises,
New horizons,
Dimples reappear.

Black rivers
Wash scales from my eyes
To see the unseen.

Soul watered,
Rest follows.
I am still,
All that lies within.[21]

CHAPTER 8

The Gift of Joy – Unleashed Gratitude

How can we know what joy is without having suffered?

HANDS

Burning pain seized my entire body. Heat beamed out of my hands like the hot blue flames radiating from a gas stove. For three weeks, I had used my arms and hands to transfer my body from chair to toilet to wheelchair to bed, and they just weren't having it anymore. I couldn't even lift a small paper cup, and I couldn't use my feet because my heels felt as if they were pierced with corkscrews, so to the ER we went.

The emergency room doctor did my intake report, then stepped out of the room to cry the tears she held back while I answered her questions. I wanted to go to the nurse's station to console her, but I couldn't move. She saw my brokenness—that I could use neither my hands nor my feet. And I saw her brokenness—she didn't have a remedy for me except a useless one-night stay in the hospital. The orthopedic hand specialist told me he didn't know if my hand functions could be restored.

Every moment was excruciating. Every second was a second too long to endure. I sat in a chair by my bedroom window for two long months and wept. My hands and feet burned like the blue flames of a fire that refused to be quenched. Mark sat beside me, drying my tears. He fed me, read to me, cried with me, emptied my commode, and held all my pieces together. He hardly left my side.

As I sat there, I watched people walk along the trail behind our house. I wondered if any of them even knew to be grateful for their ability to walk. I looked at the homes all around and wondered what brokenness was lurking inside each. All of us are broken in different ways, and each house has its own story. I prayed for them as I sat by my window. All I could do was pray and keep enduring.

In the Black

Tears pouring,
Pain ignoring
Presence of a God.
Alone in a place not known,
Yet mine to own,
A place where the darkest of darkness grows darker still.
Spiraling downward,
Concaving inward,
Black upon black,
Layer upon layer,
Heavy upon heavy,
Spilling into darkness deeper still.

Alone and apart from myself
Mystified by pain,
Nowhere to go but spinning out of control.
I am still, but I cannot stop.
Pulled under, I cannot breathe.

Fear grips, strangles, freezes;
Cold and numb.

Feeling no feeling outside of pain
I am empty, but full
Of fear
Alone in the darkness of my soul,
Desirous of death.

For no one can endure this pain.
No one can withstand this pressure
Of the darkness inside the pain.

Darkness thuds through my veins
Blackness colors my matter darker than gray.
What matters anyway?
My hands, my feet,
Spikes pierce through.
My God, my God, why have you forsaken me?
Shake me so I'll awake
From this terror of night.

Imprisoned in the cells of this body,
Heart pulsating to the offbeat of a broken drum.
I am summoned to a place I've never been,
Where no one should have to go.
But I am here.
Alone.
In the black.[22]

TWO YEARS LATER – THE YEAR 2020

I have never been one to raise a hand toward God at church. I've never had anything against hand-raisers, I've just never been comfortable doing that myself.

I don't know if you've ever lost complete use of your hands, but if you have, you know you become keenly aware of all they do for you and others. I suddenly had a lot of time to think about the functions and intricacies of this marvelous extremity—for instance, the ability to unscrew a water bottle, to point, wash my hair, pump a hair spray bottle, pet the dog, peel wrapping paper off a gift, and write a card. I also learned more about the anatomy and physiology of the hand.

- The hand has 27 bones—one-quarter of all the bones in the body!
- Thirty muscles in the hand work together in astoundingly complex ways.
- The thenar eminence muscles at the base of the thumb enable the thumb and tips of the four fingers to touch each other.
- The hypothenar eminence muscles control the little finger's movement, allowing us to move it in and out.
- There are short muscles between the metacarpal bones (on top of your fist) in the fingers, which allow us to stretch them and pull them back together.
- There are also worm-like muscles called lumbricals that help bend joints and extend the fingers.
- Extensor tendons stretch the hand and run through the back of the hand to the fingers' tips.
- Flexor tendons run through the palms to the fingers.
- Tendon sheaths act as a lubricant, which allows tendons to slide smoothly.
- Two major arteries supply the hand with blood—one on

the side of the thumb and the other—you guessed it, on the pinky side.

- The radial nerve, ulnar nerve, and median nerve provide sensations to different parts of the hand.
- There are 17,000 touch receptors and free nerve endings in the palm.
- The skin on the fingers is especially sensitive to touch.[23]

We use our hands in countless ways, most of the time unaware of all they do. One way we use our hands is to express excitement:

- We raise our arms and hands collectively in metachronal rhythm at a ballgame to create "the wave."
- We raise parallel arms straight up, symbolizing goalposts as we shout, "Touch down!"
- We do the pumped fist pull-down as we yell or whisper "YESSS!" in celebration after a promotion or landing a date.
- We raise our pointer finger toward the heavens and shout, "We're #1!" after winning a championship game.
- We raise our hands and sway in unison to the music with fellow concertgoers.

It was then I realized I never felt free to fully express myself while singing to God. I had never raised a hand toward him, even though I felt moved by the music. I stopped my full expression of joy in the church setting because I honestly thought it was a bit over-the-top. At times, I wanted to feel free enough, but I was insecure about what others would think of me. I was thinking not about God, but about myself.

I noticed I didn't think twice about raising my hands toward the heavens to celebrate a Sunday touchdown *after* church! It just flowed naturally. I didn't stop it because someone might think it was over-the-top. So, if raising hands is a natural expression of joy in various settings, why is it sometimes looked at as bizarre for someone to do at church? It's wholly accepted at ballgames, concerts, and on the dance floor. Why then was I holding back my expression to the Almighty God, who deserves more applause and praise than any other victory or celebration at any other venue?

CHURCH

After two years of not physically being able to attend church, I was finally ready to try. Mark and I strategized. We showed up to the service a little late and slipped quietly into the room with my creaky wheelchair. We sat in our self-made row of two seats against the back wall. I listened to the sermon and sang worship songs with others for the first time in two years. When the worship team came on stage, they began singing, "What a Beautiful Name" by Hillsong Worship.[24]

As I sang the words, I found myself lifting one of my splinted injured hands as best I could with gratitude toward God. I felt unbound somehow, free from judgment and everything outside of my self-focus. My hand lifted to God because my heart so inclined me. This was between me and God—an emblem of joy and an elevated heart toward him. As I reached my injured hand toward him, I imagined him reaching back down in response to gently hold my hand in his.

My God not only created these hands, but he is regenerating them as he returns their functionality after a couple of years of uncertainty, prayer, and therapy. Once again, I can open my water bottle, type this story, cut my food, and point. My God is healing my hands, and that is something to be celebrated with more excitement than a touchdown!

It took this devastation to realize I expressively celebrate so many other things more than I do God. So now, when I am so inclined, my heart reaches through my arm and down to the 27 bones, various tendons, ligaments, arteries, skin, and nerves of my hand,

and raises it all in gratitude toward my Maker and Healer. I let his healing hands lovingly hold mine. I think it makes him smile.

My injured hands have given me insight and gratitude, which in turn has blessed me with the gift of allowing myself to feel joy and freely express praise to the One who deserves it. He has helped me find joy in my sadness. Author and therapist K. J. Ramsey agrees: "We the fellowship of the broken, become the best holders of joy."[25] Paradoxically, joy was formed in me through the darkness of suffering. Jennie Allen says about joy, "Lasting joy will come only when God is in the center; not when I am empowered but when I rest in His power."[26] How can we fully know and appreciate joy without having suffered? Joy is born from suffering.

CHAPTER 9

The Gift of Community – Air Pocket

*How can we know what community is until we
make space for others?*

THE PARALYTIC

In the Bible, when friends of a paralyzed man hear Jesus is in town,
one of them orchestrates a gathering to carry him to Jesus (Luke
5:17–26). They do not hoist him over the shoulder of one hopeful
man. Instead, at least four devoted friends pick up the corners of
his mat and rush him down the dirt roads to get him to the home
where Jesus is teaching. Crowds gather in and around the house,
but the group does not arrive fast enough. They encounter some
challenges.

But faith, hope, love, and friends work together to defeat obstacles. The friends quickly brainstorm, lift their disabled friend
onto the rooftop, kick the fiddler off, and dig a laser beam hole
right through the roof with their faith. They lower the paralyzed
man at the end of his rope with such precision that he appears to
be levitating above the best seat in the house—right smack in front
of the Teacher.

Jesus' attention is gripped as he looks up at the hopeful, sweaty
faces staring down at him. He then fixes his gaze on the eyes of the
despairing man. Jesus sees the years of compounded sorrow in his

eyes, and his compassion cannot help it. He pivots from his previous lesson to take advantage of the moment to teach a new, more important lesson. The Healer is very aware of the watching crowd. He points to Exhibit A, himself, and shows the crowd his Father had given God's Son authority to perform miracles *and* to forgive sins. He says to the paralyzed man, "Friend, your sins are forgiven" (Luke 5:20).

You should have seen the teachers of the law in the corner sneering their unspoken thoughts! "This is blasphemy! Only God can forgive sins!" Gasps interrupt the almost dead silence. Jesus knows their disbelieving thoughts and asks them, "Which is easier: to say, 'Your sins are forgiven,' or to say, 'Get up and walk?'" (Luke 5:23). This is the precise moment Jesus reveals to the people his Father has given him authority to forgive sins.

Jesus then says to the somewhat confused and still paralyzed man, "Get up, take your mat, and go home" (Luke 5:24). All eyes lock onto the man as he stirs one foot, then the other. He sits up, stands up, then bends down to fold his mat and walks trustfully toward the door to go home. Each step he takes, the crowd parts, creating a parade-like atmosphere for him to leave. Shouts of praise burst from the onlookers, praising the Son of God, saying, "I can't believe it! We've never seen anything like this before!"

By the time the man reaches the dirt road, his friends have already jumped off the roof and hoisted the fiddler back up there. They find their healed friend and leap like a herd of deer all the way home!

Then will the eyes of the blind be opened and the ears of the deaf unstopped. Then will the lame leap like a deer, and the mute tongue shout for joy. Water will gush forth in the wilderness and streams in the desert (Isa. 35:5–6).

FAITH OF FRIENDS

To be cast into the fringe of society makes you feel worthless. When I was dressed in my slick black suit with royal blue blouse and black heels, standing on stage teaching athletes the value of nutrition, I felt on top of my self-esteem mountain. I found my worth according to my knowledge and how people responded to me. I felt I was contributing something of value and neatly tucked my definition of self-worth into my suit pocket. I began falling down my self-esteem mountain as a result of my second debilitating injury. I avalanched to the base along with all the rubble to sort through. Did you know if you're buried in an avalanche, you have a 50% chance of survival?[27] All I could do was poke a little air pocket, lay there, and depend on others to dig me out.

Mark and I are friends with a community of couples with at least one spouse with a physical ailment. One evening, the women in the group gathered on a deck to discuss Jennie Allen's book, *Get Out of Your Head*. I always plan to attend these gatherings, but my will isn't always the deciding factor. Pain is. Instead of visiting on a deck that evening, I tried to float in a bathtub to relieve pressure points on my thighs and backside from sitting so much. I was also nursing some rotator cuff tears and biceps tendonitis in both arms from trying to walk with crutches for over a year.

At this point, I could not sit, I could not lay on my back or sides (sacral and nerve pain), and I could not stand (nerve and musculoskeletal pain). I had been floating in the tub filled with Epsom salts for three hours when my phone rang. "You're still in the bathtub?" asked Cathy. She had invited me earlier to join the group via Zoom, but I declined because, well, I was in the bathtub. "We wanted to pray together and missed you tonight," one of my four friends sweetly said. I was relatively new to the group, so none of them knew my disability stories.

As I recounted my stories of tumultuous pain, the water level in the bathtub rose as tears poured out. I described my debilitating accident and the domino effect of the pain affecting increasing numbers of body parts—both feet, sacrum, thighs, hips, hands, wrists, arms, and shoulders. I was helpless and desperate to reach for the end of the rope used to lower the paralyzed man down to Jesus. I literally didn't know where I could go next, but I couldn't spend the night in the bathtub. I had no place where I could position my body to decrease my pain.

Cathy, Crissie, Sunnie, and Shannon each took turns praying for me while I wept as quietly as possible so I could hear them. The one request I remember being spoken by Cathy with solid faith was, "God, please heal Darci now." I felt like I imagine the paralyzed man did as his friends surrounded him to take him to Jesus, his only hope. Jesus is my only hope. My four new friends, learning of my desperation, each grabbed a corner of that heavy-laden bathtub and brought me and their faith to God with a laser beam desperate request for healing. Following the prayer, Mark hoisted me out of the bathtub and onto the hard bed where I again cried myself to sleep in heartbreaking pain.

GEESE

The steadfast love of the LORD never ceases,
   his mercies never come to an end;
they are new every morning;
   great is thy faithfulness (Lam. 3:22–23, RSV).

When I woke up, my first thought was of geese. Not the kind flying in the sky, the kind who are down for the count and whose down is stuffed into blankets. Weird, I know, but I just went with it, kind of like the paralyzed man did when his friends blew the roof off the house and the mind of Jesus with their faith. The idea lulled me to log into the online river of package deliveries called Amazon, where I was compelled to order a goose down throw blanket. When it primly arrived two days later, Mark folded it in half and laid it on the bed to cushion me from the already padded but still too hard mattress.

Anything touching nerve pain feels hard. The $5,000 bed I was lying on was purchased (hurrah for no-interest loans) to remedy some of my nighttime pain. That stupid bed and nothing worked. That is, until my goose down blanket arrived. It worked so well I bought another to place atop other soft things already on the seat of my blazing red "Mario Kart" electric chair. If you've ever sat on one of those things, you'd realize the designer didn't think about the fact you'd be sitting on it. The down blanket softened the seat, making it a refuge from the rigidity underneath. There is a beautiful Psalm in the Bible that says,

> He will cover you with his feathers, and under his wings you will find refuge; his faithfulness will be your shield and rampart. You will not fear the terror of night, nor the arrow that flies by day, nor the pestilence that stalks in the darkness, nor the plague that destroys at midday (Ps. 91:4–6).

In *This Too Shall Last*, author K. J. Ramsey writes, "If our Savior chose to enter the human story in a human body, then we should enter one another's places of suffering remembering we carry and extend the presence of Christ."[28] Since my friends brought me to Jesus, I have not had to float like a goose on water as often. I had been getting into the bathtub nightly for three weeks. Now I nestle into the down blanket under my body, the wings of his refuge over me. I still have pain, but I have *less* pain, enabling me to function enough to sit and write this book. Thank God for the faith of a devoted group of friends. Ironically, a quote from the book the group was reading by Jennie Allen states, "Yep. A tribe, a posse, a squad changes us even physically. We were built by a communal God for community. We need this!"[29] Yes, I was changed even physically by my squad. All of us need community. If you don't feel you need community now, one day you will, so go find your tribe! They may need *you* right now.

Thank you, God, for geese—for planting that thought in my mind the morning after our group prayer. "Again, I tell you that if two of you on earth agree about anything you ask for, it will be done for you by my Father in heaven. For where two or three come together in my name, there am I with them" (Matt. 18:19-20). I had not been abandoned.

CHAPTER 10

The Gift of Transformation – A Caregiver's Perspective

By Mark Steiner

How can we be formed without carving and chiseling?
He is forming us into who he intends us to be.

My wife Darci is easy to love. She is, herself, very loving, as well as spiritual, smart, funny, kind, feisty, and beautiful. I've always loved being around her. She has been a fantastic wife, mother, daughter, sister, and friend. For our first nine years of marriage, we built a wonderful life together, with two small daughters, a house, a steady income, and positions of respect in our church.

For us, seasons of suffering have come without warning. One day Darci was an active young wife, mother, and leader, then suddenly totally disabled, writhing in pain. Days turned into years. There was nothing I could do to fix her adversity. Over time, things significantly improved. Then, years later, in the blink of an eye, it happened all over again, and once more, there have been no solutions.

It's grueling to suffer chronic pain. You might miss how hard it is for Darci because she endures far more than meets the eye. For

Darci, there are extended periods where it's painful to walk, sit, *and* lie down. Even at night, there is often little relief. It is humiliating to her that she needs help doing simple things. I know she often goes without things she needs because she doesn't want to bother me. There is gnawing fear about the future and the strain the ordeal sometimes places on our relationship. Many people treat her condescendingly or completely ignore her. It is a lonely world, even with family and friends that really want to understand.

The miraculous healing I have *hoped for* is for Darci to be freed from her suffering. The miraculous healing I have *witnessed* is how during her suffering, Darci's ordeal has transformed her. Amid her pain, she found strength to reconcile with her father and care for him wheelchair to wheelchair (with help) during his final years of life. Rather than becoming bitter and withdrawn, she found a faith that transcended her condition. When people let her down, including me, she forgives and finds consolation in her relationship with God. And as she perseveres through the years, she finds gifts and treasures from God in her trials that she longs to share with others.

THE PARABLE OF THE GOOD SAMARITAN

...he asked Jesus, "And who is my neighbor?"

Jesus replied with a story: "A Jewish man was traveling from Jerusalem down to Jericho, and he was attacked by bandits. They stripped him of his clothes, beat him up, and left him half dead beside the road.

"By chance a priest came along. But when he saw the man lying there, he crossed to the other side of the road and passed him by. A Temple assistant[a] walked over and looked at him lying there, but he also passed by on the other side.

"Then a despised Samaritan came along, and when he saw the man, he felt compassion for him. Going over to him, the

Samaritan soothed his wounds with olive oil and wine and bandaged them. Then he put the man on his own donkey and took him to an inn, where he took care of him. The next day he handed the innkeeper two silver coins, telling him, 'Take care of this man. If his bill runs higher than this, I'll pay you the next time I'm here.'

"Now which of these three would you say was a neighbor to the man who was attacked by bandits?" Jesus asked.

The man replied, "The one who showed him mercy."

Then Jesus said, "Yes, now go and do the same."

(Luke 10:29–37, NLT).

I think about this story often. I can identify with every character in the tale, including the donkey. At times I've been compassionate like the Good Samaritan. But like the priest, sometimes I make really "spiritual" excuses not to care for her. Like the Temple assistant, I think the priest up ahead (spiritual leader) neglects her and I get critical. Like the innkeeper, I've sometimes treated her like a tenant, providing food and shelter without really being connected. And like the donkey, I don't think anyone cares or appreciates how heavy my burden is.

Very few people know what it is like, or how to offer encouragement and support. Sometimes, I reach the end of my rope and can't do it anymore. I tell people it can be like holding your hand in a flame. I suspect each caregiver has their own version of burnout. Some caregivers leave. Others turn to other sources of fulfillment, like affairs, alcohol, or work. My version is to "go zombie." I grow cold toward her, go through the motions, and grumble. It's odd how quickly I can go from caring about how my suffering wife feels to focusing instead on how her suffering makes *me* feel.

Frankly, caring for someone undergoing extended suffering exposes you. It brings out the truth about who you are—not the person everyone around you thinks you are, but the real you. It also reveals a lot about your family, your friends, your neighbors, and fellow Christians. Some people you never expected to care come to you like divine gifts. Other folks you considered compassionate, dependable, and kind aren't nearly as much that way as you thought. To be fair, you realize you aren't as much that way as you thought either.

The truth is, I'm an odd choice for a caregiver. When I was 11, my parents divorced, my brother went off to college, and my sister soon moved in with my dad. I became a classic latchkey kid. Doesn't it make more sense that growing up in a two-parent family, where the parents adore each other, would be a better foundation to become a caring husband? Doesn't it seem obvious that an intact home where love and compassion are patiently instilled in children over many years would be better preparation for selfless caregiving? It does, unless perhaps the Father, Son, and Spirit want to transform you.

It is humiliating to recall how immature and inept I was in my relationships in my early years. As a non-believer, I put my hope in politics. However, during that journey, and very unintentionally, I found myself attending a Bible study for the first time in my life. In a room full of doctors and nurses, a gray-haired man led a study of Jesus' healing of a man with leprosy.

JESUS HEALS A LEPER

A man with leprosy came to him and begged him on his knees, "If you are willing, you can make me clean." Filled with compassion, Jesus reached out his hand and touched the man. "I am willing," he said. "Be clean!" Immediately the leprosy left him, and he was cleansed (Mark 1:40–42).

The elderly man looked up and repeated, "The compassion of Christ." With a heart that reflected these very words, he repeated it again and again, "*The compassion of Christ ...*"

This man and the group around him knew a great deal about suffering and compassion; they were treating orphans and refugees from the Khmer Rouge "killing fields" and the fighting between Cambodian guerillas and the Vietnamese army on the border of Cambodia and Thailand. *The compassion of Christ.* What could better heal the wounds of the world, of the Cambodian refugees, of a deeply hurting young man like me, than the compassion of Christ? Shortly thereafter, I committed my life to Jesus.

Twenty years later, I was again learning the need for the compassion of Christ in a very personal way. I had become convinced Darci was going to die. Her condition had been rapidly worsening, her pain spiraling out of control, and my strength and hope were gone. One night, I walked into the darkness and tried to accept the prospect of my life, and the lives of our two little girls, without her. As my heart was breaking, a transforming realization took shape within me. I would rather suffer anything on Darci's behalf than lose her. I now believe that was the Spirit of Christ within me, calling me to lay down my life for her as he had for me.

As another twenty years have passed, being Darci's companion in suffering is teaching me how to love better. At my worst, I still "numb out" and withdraw from her. At my best, compassion fills my heart. I face her sorrow and pain and share in it. I stay connected and give her my heart. I focus on her pain, not mine. I delight in giving to her creatively, repeatedly. Ironically, we have become more emotionally intimate and bonded in the hardships than we have ever been before.

It helps enormously that I found a wise mentor. He helps me accept that, because of the image of God and the power of the Holy

Spirit within me, I can love like Christ. Darci and I have also been led to a community of believers who openly share similar struggles and support one another.

As Christ frees us from our selfishness, we can give more freely. Focusing on giving without expectations of gratitude or getting anything in return is a wonderful freedom to have. So much of giving in our world is transactional, full of ulterior motives. Yet there is a purity, holiness in giving unconditionally. God showers us with blessings we don't deserve and don't even notice. He does it out of love, out of humility, because that is who he is. I want to be more like him. That kind of love is contagious. It reflects him and unleashes his image that he instills within us.

My experience as a caregiver has suggested something very profound to me: Like humility, love and compassion are a path, not a destination. Somehow the peaks and valleys of caring for a sufferer fit together. There is a never-ending battle between the selfish flesh and the image of Christ within me. By admitting my selfishness, pride drains from my heart, and there is room for love and compassion. I have something to give, with no strings attached, and Christ is displayed in me. Then, over time, compassion drains from my heart, and self again fills the void.

Eventually, I recognize my selfishness and realize my own need for the compassion of Christ. He patiently refills my heart with a love that demands nothing and expects nothing in return. The cycle repeats itself, and hopefully, over time, my life is transforming into a better reflection of his.

A note from Darci: In the *Study Guide for Beauty Beyond the Thorns: Discovering Gifts in Suffering* are some specific ideas of how you can help encourage or take care of a caregiver.

CHAPTER 11

The Gift of Faith – A Meteorologist's Faith

*How can we know how to have faith
without learning from others who embody it?*

THE FAITH OF THE CENTURION

When Jesus had entered Capernaum, a centurion came to him, asking for help. "Lord," he said, "my servant lies at home paralyzed, suffering terribly." Jesus said to him, "Shall I come and heal him?" The centurion replied, "Lord, I do not deserve to have you come under my roof. But just say the word, and my servant will be healed. For I myself am a man under authority, with soldiers under me. I tell this one, 'Go,' and he goes; and that one, 'Come,' and he comes. I say to my servant, 'Do this,' and he does it." When Jesus heard this, he was amazed and said to those following him, "Truly I tell you, I have not found anyone in Israel with such great faith. I say to you that many will come from the east and the west and will take their places at the feast with Abraham, Isaac and Jacob in the kingdom of heaven. But the subjects of the kingdom will be thrown outside, into the darkness, where there will be weeping and gnashing of teeth." Then Jesus said to the centurion, "Go! Let it be done just as you believed it would." And his servant was healed at that moment (Matt. 8:5–13).

CENTURIAN'S SERVANT

In amazement, Jesus said he had not found anyone in Israel with such great faith. But the centurion was a Roman! An outsider! A Gentile! He was one of the first Gentiles to put his faith in Jesus.

Imagine what it would be like if Jesus commended the depth of your faith, telling you it surpasses that of anyone in the country, including that of the religious leaders! The centurion's faith was genuine, unlike the Pharisees. The centurion was a military officer in charge of one hundred men in a Roman legion. Despite his authority, in humility, he recognized Jesus as having greater authority than himself and called Jesus "Lord." Not only that, but he recognized he was not worthy for someone with such great power to even enter his home. Jesus sent his command from afar to heal the servant, just like the Roman centurion *knew he could*, and the servant was healed at that moment.

MOSTLY SUNNY

If you are from Denver, you may remember meteorologist Pam Daale, who forecasted the weather for a major local channel from 1993 to 2003. During her stint there, she became chief meteorologist. In 2002, Pam was diagnosed with breast cancer. She recovered, then battled its ravages again in 2004, until she died from it at age 40. Pam had beautifully manicured, above-the-shoulder blonde hair, which she lost during chemotherapy treatment. While on-air, Pam sometimes wore a wig or a colorful head wrap, and sometimes she reported the weather with nothing to cover her baldness. She wrote an online public journal during her bout with cancer that was later bound into a book, *Mostly Sunny, Partly Cloudy*. That's how Pam was—mostly sunny.

One of the most remarkable things about Pam is she also had paraplegia. At 16, during a solo ride, her horse reared and fell on her, severing her spine. She waited, face up in a golden field in Iowa, until her family came looking for her.

The station had ramps built to accommodate her disability. She was a pro at maneuvering her wheelchair while also pointing to the green screen.

I became friends with Pam while she was fighting her first battle with cancer. Our young daughters were friends at school. I was recovering from my earlier disability and approached her on foot while picking up our daughters from school. Pam was not easy to disguise. She had on a head wrap and sunglasses, but the wheelchair was the giveaway. While chatting, we set a time to get together the next day so the girls could play. Pam moved about her house caring for the needs of her daughter and two-year-old son without a hitch. She never acted disabled.

During future playdates, we sat around her kitchen table getting to know one another. She told me about her horse fall and how she never panicked, even though she couldn't move. She prayed peacefully to God, facing the heavens, fully trusting him. Peace doesn't come from the absence of pain—peace comes from spending time with God.

Sometimes the radiation to eradicate the cancer left burning red rash marks on Pam's body and neck. These bothered her, but television has good make-up crews. She told me she was often cold without her hair, but her cat sensed her need and laid on her head at night, never having done that before. We spoke of her favorite verses in the Bible that comforted her. I can't remember her favorite, but maybe that's because I don't have the whole Bible memorized.

Pam couldn't go into many people's homes because few have ramps, but mine did. My ramp was steep, and I watched her muscular biceps and triceps flex to their maximum capacities. She struggled up the ramp, idled at times, but would not let me help push her. Sheer mental determination controlled those arm muscles. I saw it in her face and took note. She wouldn't let anyone help her with anything she could do herself.

Pam had more humility and faith in God than anyone I have ever met. She was like the centurion Jesus commended. She knew Jesus was the answer, so she put her faith in him. She stayed positive and engaged in life with her husband and two small children. I never saw her down, although I'm sure she lamented before God. One afternoon, after looking at some Bible verses together, I expressed my sorrow for her struggles. After I finished my heartfelt discourse, Pam, with her injured body, bald head, and sunken blue eyes, looked at me so innocently, and she said, "You know, I really don't think I have it that bad." I had gone over to Pam's house to encourage her faith. Her faith wasn't in need of strengthening, mine was. I handed her my Bible and asked her to teach me how to trust God the way she did.

In her online journal, she spoke of her faith and trust in God. He was her hope and her healer. To her, she was already healed because she was forgiven. And she was right. We celebrated together when doctors determined she had defeated the cancer! When her hair began growing back, curly and darker this time, she embraced it and continued reporting the weather.

One April morning, I called Pam to see if I could come over for a visit. She didn't pick up, so I left a message. Her husband called me back and said Pam's cancer had returned with a vengeance. He asked if I could watch the kids the next day. Of course, I would have, but it was my little sister DaNia's wedding day. Pam died while I was at the wedding.

Her memorial service was packed. I sat with the other moms from the elementary school. This woman of faith profoundly impacted the lives of everyone there and throughout the state of Colorado who watched her report "Sunny with a few clouds" instead of "Partly cloudy." This television personality fought every stage of cancer on a public stage with courage. She did not fear the thoughts of other people, and they embraced her bravery. Pam's wheelchair sat on the stage during the memorial service. Pam was no longer confined to it; I bet she was riding her horse in heavenly fields of gold.

Pam's faith lives on in me; her life has helped heal a lot of mistrust in my life. God uses faithful people to help faithless people. God gifted me deeper trust in him as a result of watching Pam live out her faith. God also gifted faith to those watching the Roman centurion trust in Jesus.

Yes, I am back in my wheelchair, but I have an example set before me who showed me how to believe that difficulties are to heal deeper needs we aren't even aware of. Pam showed me that despite problems, life is still "mostly sunny."

CHAPTER 12

The Gift of Mercy – Mr. Miyagi

How can we know what mercy is until we've practiced gifting it?

JAYWALKING

The police officer pulled over, lights flashing, and issued me a ticket. Seriously? I had lived in Los Angeles for only a few days and was just issued a ticket for jaywalking! I had spent the day job hunting in my red dress and black J. C. Penney pumps, and I was heading over to Mark's apartment after exiting my last bus of the day. Man, did my feet ever hurt! I walked in hose-covered feet, dangling my pumps from a couple of fingers by my side until I reached a bizarre street that T-boned an entrance to a small dark alley. There was a stoplight there for no apparent reason, and it seemed to not want to turn green, so I crossed. There was no one in sight, except for a hidden, unmarked police car, I would soon discover.

I don't know, maybe I looked suspicious walking barefoot. I was wobbling a bit in pain, too, which may have made me appear slightly intoxicated. I told the police officer my story, but he had no mercy. None. How was crossing at the crosswalk jaywalking, anyway? It's just a hunch, but I think there were way worse infractions occurring in L.A. that this hidden police officer could have been spending his time writing citations for.

(*Note:* I am grateful for police officers who put their lives on the line to sustain law and order. I am using this story to merely demonstrate a point, not because I'm ungrateful for their protection).

MR. MIYAGI

In the movie, *Karate Kid Part II*, as Daniel and his sensei Mr. Miyagi are leaving a karate tournament, they witness Daniel's competitor Johnny being choked by his own sensei, Cobra Kai. Mr. Miyagi approaches this dangerous situation to help Johnny. Cobra Kai gets angry when he sees Miyagi and lets go of Johnny to fight Miyagi. Miyagi, in his wisdom, avoids two punches to the face which cause Cobra Kai to punch each of his fists through two separate car windows, shattering them. His hands bleeding, Cobra Kai yells in terror as Miyagi grabs him by the coat and pretends to go for his jugular. The wide-eyed look on Cobra Kai is comically terrifying.

Miyagi, with his Japanese accent, repeats Cobra Kai's slogan: "Mercy is for the weak. We do not train to be merciful here. When man face you, he is enemy. Enemy deserves no mercy." Miyagi stops his hand midair and instead gently squeezes Cobra Kai's nose making a honking noise. He then lets go of Cobra Kai, who falls to the ground exhausted but alive.

As Daniel and Miyagi leave, Daniel says, "You could have killed him, couldn't you have? Why didn't you then?" Miyagi says, "Because Daniel-san, a person with no forgiveness in heart, live in even worse punishment than death."[30] Mr. Miyagi demonstrated to Daniel, Cobra Kai, Johnny, and the others an example of mercy.

The Pharisees pounced on Jesus, waiting to catch him disobeying the law so they could arrest him. They were like Cobra Kai, whose motto was, "Strike first. Strike hard. No mercy." The Pharisees resented Jesus every time he healed on the Sabbath, but Jesus loved, extended mercy, and cured at least seven people on the Sabbath, freeing them from their infirmities so *they* could finally have rest.

Hypocritically, the Pharisees went to work on the Sabbath, conspiring how to kill this merciful Healer. Jesus showed everyone that doing good, like saving a life, was an exception to the law, and the law never intended such ridiculous rigidity.

> Woe to you, teachers of the law and Pharisees, you hypocrites! You give a tenth of your spices—mint, dill and cumin. But you have neglected the more important matters of the law—justice, mercy and faithfulness. You should have practiced the latter, without neglecting the former (Matt. 23:23).

VIPERS, COBRAS, SERPENTS

When I finally made it to Mark's place after my unexpected visit with the police officer, Mark showed me *his* ticket. Apparently, the moving van was not welcome in L.A. either. We knew living in Los Angeles would be costlier than Colorado, but we hadn't anticipated racking up over $300 in fines during our first week there. We were still unemployed, and California was not making it easy for us to eat, and I'm not kidding. We had no money and were extended no mercy for rules we didn't know we were breaking.

What do vipers, cobras, and serpents have in common? They are out to kill. Jesus aptly called the Pharisees a "brood of vipers" because they were out to kill him. Cobra Kai said, "The enemy deserves no mercy." He and his assembly were out to kill. And the serpent Satan was out to obliterate Jesus. Satan still roams the earth looking for whom next to spiral, suffocate, and devour (1 Peter 5:8). He is not a fictional tale. Oh no. He is out to kill us too, people! Living the truths of the Bible are how we fight back, and we must, or we will be misled into his prideful, selfish, and hateful way of life.

Satan will always be out to get us, trap us, devour us. We need to watch and be aware of his schemes. He hides in temptation, hissing in our ear for us to follow our self-indulgent desires, which will in time make us more like him.

Jesus urges us to be humble and grant mercy even when we are wronged, just like Mr. Miyagi extended to Cobra Kai. "Blessed are the merciful, for they will be shown mercy" (Matt. 5:7). We can forgive others more easily when we recognize our deep, personal need to be forgiven ourselves. Be a peacemaker. Holding grudges hurts you. Forgive. Extend mercy. Everyone is going through something difficult.

Who comes to mind that you need to forgive and grant mercy? Not because they deserve it, but because your heart, health, and spirit need it. God will show *you* mercy in return. What are the benefits of granting mercy and forgiveness when you've been wronged and have suffered? *Receiving* mercy and forgiveness yourself. As Mr. Miyagi says, "A person with no forgiveness in heart live in even worse punishment than death."[31]

- Speak and act as those who are going to be judged by the law that gives freedom, because judgment without mercy will be shown to anyone who has not been merciful. Mercy triumphs over judgment (James 2:12–13).
- Blessed are the peacemakers, for they will be called children of God (Matt. 5:9).

CHAPTER 13

The Gift of Repentance – Walking Toward the Cross

How can we know what repentance is until we walk toward the cross instead of a comfortable life?

FORGIVENESS

I used to work for a criminal in Beverly Hills. He was not prosecuted until 2011, but ten years prior, I wrote dictation and assisted this man in setting up offshore banks. He had also been arrested in 1972 and served prison time for theft in other business dealings. His 2011 indictment was for selling illegal offshore banks. The IRS had investigated him for some time, and in 2011 they finally imprisoned him for swindling clients of millions of dollars. "The information highway" (internet) was in developmental stages, and had I access to research his background before accepting a job from him, I would have declined the job, thank you very much.

No matter, he fired me anyway. I caught the flu from his assistant and missed two days of work just like she had, but he was far from sympathetic. I went into work, still a little green and nauseous, and was handed my last paycheck. I almost threw up on his diamond-studded Jason of Beverly Hills shoes. Instead, I walked down Beverly Boulevard in my J. C. Penney heels, holding my teeny paycheck, wondering how Mark and I were going to get married in three weeks. I *was* thankful for this job because it fed me. Two months earlier, while job hunting in downtown Los Angeles, I had stood in front of a Burger King, inhaling the aroma of charbroiled meat, crying. I was hungry. I had no money. I survived by stealing bites of my roommate's leftover couscous from the fridge. I was a thief too.

Great, just great. I didn't know we were scamming people of millions. I'm not sure where my share went. Probably to his diamond-studded shoes. In all seriousness, his firing of me protected me from further participating in illegal offshore banking deals. I did not know I was working for a prosecutable, nefarious man, even though he was pretty scary when he barked out his dictation at me.

MATTHEW

When Matthew was called to follow Jesus, he was a tax collector under the Roman government, scamming Jewish people of copious amounts of money. The Roman Empire was oppressive and corrupt. In Israel, tax collectors were thieves. They collected required Roman taxes then tacked on more to live the high life. They lived a filthy rich lifestyle on embezzled money. Emphasis on filthy.

Matthew had seen Jesus perform miracles, so when Jesus invited him to join his ministry, Matthew followed. He repented by turning away from his wealth and instead gave his life to become a disciple of Jesus.

Matthew defrauded a multitude of people and lived a life of luxury, as did my former boss. But Matthew's life changed drastically when he followed the homeless man instead of his wealth. He chose honesty over fraud and humility over prosperity. He walked next to Jesus as a student to learn about this curious upside-down way of life.

A CHOICE

Sometimes suffering comes from decisions we make. We can become spiritually sick and possibly physically ill due to bad choices. Suppose we choose lying, greed, sexual immorality, idolatry, hatred, jealousy, addiction, pornography, and the like. In these cases, we are causing our own suffering. We may not suffer immediate consequences, but at some point, they will catch up to us just like they did to my former boss. Evil contributes to its demise.

- Whoever is pregnant with evil conceives trouble and gives birth to disillusionment. Whoever digs a hole and scoops it out falls into the pit they have made. The trouble they cause recoils on them; their violence comes down on their own heads (Ps. 7:14-16).
- The Lord is not slow in keeping his promise, as some understand slowness. Instead, he is patient with you, not wanting anyone to perish, but everyone to come to repentance (2 Peter 3:9).

We all sin, but if we choose to marinade ourselves in it, we will smell more like the stench of Satan than the aroma of Christ.

GUARANTEED SUFFERING

Ironically, living a Christian life guarantees suffering too. Either way, we suffer. So why not stay living it up in a self-centered lifestyle? Because of relationship. A loving relationship with God on earth, eternal life in heaven, and an inheritance are waiting for those who choose to suffer *for* Christ instead of suffering *from* the consequences of sin. Blessings are gifts from our Father—not earned—they are gifted. Gifts are not the reason we follow Christ; we follow Christ because of love. Once we are in a relationship with him, we are children of his, and to his children, he gives gifts, which include attributes of himself and an eternal inheritance.

YOU DID FOR ME

I wonder which prison my former boss is in. God, who is rich in mercy, wants us to forgive those who have hurt us. And he wants us to care for those imprisoned (Heb. 13:3). I wish I could talk to him now. I wish I had the courage back then to introduce him to Jesus. Anyone can come to repentance, and when you are confined in a small prison cell, it would make you think, you know? My former boss is not beyond hope of restoration. None of us are. We are to forgive because we too need forgiveness (Matt. 6:14–15). All of us are guilty of sin. It is Jesus who shows us the way to forgive. Matthew chose to be a lowly sheep and gave up his wealth that didn't satisfy. What he gained in his repentance is priceless and eternal. We would do well to follow his example. One day, we will be separated by the King into the classification of a sheep or a goat.

SHEEP AND THE GOATS:

When the Son of Man comes in his glory, and all the angels with him, he will sit on his glorious throne. All the nations will be gathered before him, and he will separate the people one from another as a shepherd separates the sheep from the goats. He will put the sheep on his right and the goats on his left.

Then the King will say to those on his right, "Come, you who are blessed by my Father; take your inheritance, the kingdom prepared for you since the creation of the world. For I was hungry and you gave me something to eat, I was thirsty and you gave me something to drink, I was a stranger and you invited me in, I needed clothes and you clothed me, I was sick and you looked after me, I was in prison and you came to visit me."

Then the righteous will answer him, "Lord, when did we see you hungry and feed you, or thirsty and give you something to drink? When did we see you a stranger and invite you in, or needing clothes and clothe you? When did we see you sick or in prison and go to visit you?"

The King will reply, "Truly I tell you, whatever you did for one of the least of these brothers and sisters of mine, you did for me."

Then he will say to those on his left, "Depart from me, you who are cursed, into the eternal fire prepared for the devil and his angels. For I was hungry and you gave me nothing to eat, I was thirsty and you gave me nothing to drink, I was a stranger and you did not invite me in, I needed clothes and you did not clothe me, I was sick and in prison and you did not look after me."

They also will answer, "Lord, when did we see you hungry or thirsty or a stranger or needing clothes or sick or in prison, and did not help you?"

He will reply, "Truly I tell you, whatever you did not do for one of the least of these, you did not do for me."

Then they will go away to eternal punishment, but the righteous to eternal life (Matt. 25:31–46).

CHAPTER 14

The Gift of Endurance – Purer Than Gold

*How can we know what endurance is
without being refined by fire?*

SMILES

I turned the key to enter my apartment, slipped off my pumps and climbed onto the bed crying out to God for a new job. How was I going to tell Mark I had just been fired? Mascara was everywhere except on my eyelashes—I didn't know I'd need waterproof that day.

The phone rang. I told God I'd be back in a sec and got up to answer the landline. It was one of the temporary job agencies I'd applied at when I began my job search in Los Angeles. A Japanese entertainment company in Century City needed someone to come in to set up a filing system. After I picked up my jaw, I said, "Yes, *yes*, I'm available. I'll be there in about forty-five minutes!" I returned to the bed to finish my prayer and exclaimed, "Thank you, Jesus!"

After fixing my face, I threw on my pumps and caught a bus traveling down Olympic Boulevard to Century City. I danced off the bus and into one of the twin Century Plaza Towers. Floating up the elevator took about as long as the bus ride there. I could see the famous "*Die Hard* building" not far from there.

My new boss and I got along magnificently, and she didn't even bark dictation at me. By the end of the day, I had been hired for a permanent administrative position, even after requesting time off for my honeymoon. The employees sprinkled me with wedding wishes, and I didn't feel like throwing up anymore. My boss's boss's boss took us out to lunch so I could get to know everyone. "Thank you, Jesus," my stomach growled.

There was one problem. I don't speak Japanese.

No matter, my new co-workers all sipped their soup and smiled at me. A smile speaks every language. I felt extremely welcomed. My boss's boss spoke fairly good English, so she communicated what I needed to know and taught me "konnichiwa," a Japanese greeting. At one point she leaned over to whisper in my ear, "dennisharpa" while very non-discretely pointing to the guy sitting across the table from me. I could not understand her, so leaned in for a repeat. In the meantime, the guy flipped up his sunglasses and smiled at me. Sure enough, I ate lunch with Dennis Hopper, and didn't even get his autograph. I didn't even say, "Hey, I loved your role in Hoosiers!" Instead, I ate my egg roll, not quite sure what to do with Mr. Hopper and ten new Japanese friends all smiling at me. That day I was fired then hired within the same hour. Mark would never believe me, especially the part about my new name, Darci-san.

NEW NAMES

Jesus likes to give people nicknames, according to who he sees us *becoming*. Like to Simon, he gave the name Peter, meaning the "Rock," even though Peter was not rock-solid (Matt. 16:18). God saw who he was becoming instead of focusing on his weaknesses. And you know what? Peter eventually died a martyr's death for his beloved friend and Savior, and he chose to be crucified upside-down. What kind of faith is more rock-solid than that? He must have had a compelling reason to give his life in this way. He understood the "why."

What name would you like to be called by God? How do you see him forming you? I want him to call me Joy. My first name is Darci, which means "a dark dwelling place." But my middle name is Joy. I choose Joy. Wouldn't you? God is forming you and me through trials to become more like him. He knows the way there is through purification. He knows you are worth more than pure gold.

GOLD

Gold is purified by heating it at high temperatures to separate the impurities (dross) from the pure metal. During the heating, dross rises to the top and is skimmed off. Living a Christian life is like experiencing this continual purification process to become like the people Jesus speaks about in the Beatitudes. We must endure the fire to be purified—it shows us what we are made of. We cannot grow without troubles, but God has not abandoned us. Pastor Timothy Keller explains, "Suffering can refine us rather than destroy us because God himself walks in the fire with us,"[32] just like he walked in the fiery furnace with Shadrach, Meshach, and Abednego (Dan. 3:1–30).

We may never know the reason God allows us to endure the flames. Job never understood the "why" in his suffering. God never told him, even though they conversed. If God had described to Job the reason for his suffering, Job wouldn't have exemplified his faith the way he did by *not* knowing.[33] Millions of people who read his story would not be impacted to the degree we are by his battle with severe difficulties, unimaginable losses, and fiery pain. Sure, Job complained to God and got angry with him, but he fought through his suffering with honest prayer—he never stopped praying. He just got mad. I get mad too.

ENDURANCE

Moving to Los Angeles without jobs was hard on Mark and me. We were asked by our church leaders to move to the Beverly Hills area, which we thought would be financially impossible. But there it was, our affordable, pink, bug-infested apartment in the 90210 ZIP Code. I hope we were more valuable volunteers for the church plant than I think we were. During our four years there, we struggled financially, through hunger, through the Northridge Earthquake, through the 1992 Los Angeles riots, and through major flooding and fires. Enduring suffering can become a gift because it is an opportunity for us to grow from who we are into who God intends for us to become. He uses suffering to form us. God used our suffering during those years to bond our marriage and prepare us for even greater pains he knew we'd have to endure in our future.

And let us run with perseverance the race marked out for us, fixing our eyes on Jesus, the pioneer and perfecter of faith. For the joy set before him he endured the cross, scorning its shame, and sat down at the right hand of the throne of God. Consider him who endured such opposition from sinners, so that you will not grow weary and lose heart (Heb. 12:1–3).

CHAPTER 15

The Gift of Direction – Dirt Roads

How can we know what direction to go when we do not have control of our steps? Our plans get thwarted, but from God's perspective, our path always points to him—True North.

THE DIRT ROAD

The dirt road was meandering, washboard bumpy, and dusty, but we were almost there. We were on our way to have dinner with some friends who lived in the quiet countryside. It was a pleasant getaway with our young family. Jennifer was nine months old and strapped sweetly and safely into her car seat in the back.

While enjoying the scenery, out of nowhere, we saw and heard a car up ahead careening out of control, kicking up dust and racing our way *fast*. Mark drove closer to the edge of the road to try to avoid getting hit. I turned around to reach for our baby, and we were fiercely T-boned. Someone in the sparsely populated neighborhood heard the crash and called 9-1-1. The seatbelt sliced through my skin on my collarbone, and I had a weird whiplash from my turned position, but the country road didn't take me home [to heaven] quite yet.

Mark was okay as he braced himself on the steering wheel. He checked on me and told me to wait for the ambulance. Jen was bleeding from the mouth. The impact forced her tiny teeth to bite into her tongue.

In the other car were three teenagers—two passengers, and the driver, a 16-year-old who we later learned received his license a week before the accident. When I saw the boys get out of the car uninjured, I unstrapped myself, went around the car to unstrap Jenny, picked her up, and handed our little nine-month-old, bleeding baby to the driver. I should have stayed put, but I was furious. As the reckless driver held Jen in his arms, I wanted him to touch a life he could have taken. I wanted to teach him a lesson. He could have killed our baby.

The ambulance came, checked Jenny, put me on a stretcher, and off I went. We filed the police report with our account of the accident, which the boy's lawyer fought against, somehow blaming us for the crash. Okay, whatever. Anyway, we were awarded money from the settlement which would pay for nutrition school. I received my books for my master's program about a month before my next accident—my fall down the stairs. School would have to be put on hold indefinitely.

VENGENCE

It is not my job to take vengeance to teach someone a lesson. "It is mine to avenge; I will repay [says the Lord]" (Deut. 32:35). I took teaching the teen driver a lesson into my own hands instead of trusting the Lord to do so. Retribution made me feel good. I wanted him to feel pain for the pain he caused us. An eye for an eye. But God says:

Do not repay anyone evil for evil. Be careful to do what is right in the eyes of everyone. If it is possible, as far as it depends on you, live at peace with everyone. Do not take revenge, my dear friends, but leave room for God's wrath, for it is written: "It is mine to avenge; I will repay," says the Lord. On the contrary: "If your enemy is hungry, feed him; if he is thirsty, give him something to drink. In doing this, you will heap burning coals on his head." Do not be overcome by evil, but overcome evil with good (Rom. 12:17–21).

In hindsight, I could have asked the boys if they were okay or given them bottles of water from our stash. I didn't care about what they just went through; I was thinking only of my family. I'm sure the driver was scared, and instead of pouring salt into his wound, I should have shown concern by extending sympathy, being thankful the three boys were not injured.

CHANGE IN DIRECTION

Our accident on that country road led me down a different path than I would have chosen. God has given me passions I never dreamed I'd have. Me, a nutritionist? Never. But yep, I studied with motivation to help myself get better. Had we not been in that accident, I wouldn't have had the money to go back to school, and I wouldn't have become a nutritionist. Learning nutrition and changing my diet have helped me recover from several of my physical ailments. God has worked everything for my good in the past, so when I doubt he will in my future, I must look back and remember his faithfulness.

> I remember my affliction and my wandering,
>   the bitterness and the gall.
> I well remember them,
>   and my soul is downcast within me.
> Yet this I call to mind
>   and therefore I have hope:
> Because of the LORD's great love we are not consumed,

for his compassions never fail.
They are new every morning;
    great is your faithfulness.
I say to myself, "The LORD is my portion;
    therefore I will wait for him" (Lam. 3:19–24).

FROM SAUL TO PAUL

"Saul, Saul, why do you persecute me?"[34] The direction of Saul's life was also changed on a dirt road. The New Testament Saul was a Pharisee who persecuted, imprisoned, and killed Christians. That is, until the risen Christ flashed a bright light around him and spoke audibly to him on his journey to Damascus. When Saul stood up, he was blinded. Jesus told him to go into the city and there he would be told what to do. The men traveling with Saul led him to the city, where he remained blind and fasted for three days.

Jesus had a new role for Saul—to preach the gospel. Ananias, a disciple, was instructed by Jesus to go to Saul and place his hands on him so that Saul could receive the Holy Spirit and his sight could be restored. Saul got up, was baptized, and began preaching that Jesus was the Son of God.

Later, after his conversion, Saul's name was changed to Paul. Paul was given a thorn in his flesh to keep him from becoming conceited. At some point, Jesus had taken him up to Paradise, but he was not to speak of it or feel conceited that God gave him this revelation. Jesus preached fervently against pride, arrogance, and conceit during his ministry because of the damage it causes. For example, Satan got kicked out of heaven because he became conceited about his beauty; Adam and Eve desired to know everything like God; and the Pharisees thought they were better than everyone else. What kept Paul from becoming conceited was pain. A thorn in his flesh was a *gift* given by God to Paul to protect him like thorns protect a rose:

So to keep me from becoming conceited because of the surpassing greatness of the revelations, a thorn was given me in the flesh, a messenger of Satan to harass me, to keep me from becoming conceited. Three times I pleaded with the Lord about this, that it should leave me. But he said to me, "My grace is sufficient for you, for my power is made perfect in weakness." Therefore I will boast all the more gladly of my weaknesses, so that the power of Christ may rest upon me. For the sake of Christ, then, I am content with weaknesses, insults, hardships, persecutions, and calamities. For when I am weak, then I am strong (2 Cor. 12:7–10).

Christ's power is made perfect in weakness. Humility is our strength that leaves room for God's grace to be sufficient. There is beauty beyond the thorns—Christ. He has reasons to allow thorns in our lives. Paul wrote more books in the Bible than anyone despite his fleshly thorn. Isn't that beautiful? See how God used Paul's thorn for good? He wants to turn our weaknesses to strengths.

Pride is more dangerous than a thorn. If you've been given a thorn, it is for your protection; it has been gifted because there is something beautiful that is being purposed for you. God knows the "why." His grace and knowledge are sufficient. You can trust him. Suffering has taught me what matters most in life is not what we see, but what God sees.

CHAPTER 16

The Gift of Fulfillment – Food and Addictions Do Not Fulfill

How can we know what fulfillment is until we let God alone fill?

NUTRITION COUNSELING

After opening my nutritional counseling practice, I learned that nutrition counseling often has more to do with counseling than nutrition. One of my earliest clients was a teenager who struggled with anorexia and had just been released from a hospital program that failed her. Let's call her Taylor. We worked from the inside out, starting with the underlying issues that made her not want to eat. Pretty quickly, it was evident that Taylor's lack of eating was a family issue, so we met with her parents.

CONTROL

Control is why many people with anorexia don't eat.[35] Not eating is something they can control when they feel out of control. I understood one reason Taylor was anorexic after meeting with her mom, who controlled *everything* in her life. Taylor needed space to make her own decisions—she was 16. Her mom backed off once she realized how her behavior was contributing to her daughter's health issues.

I taught Taylor how to cook healthy meals. She shopped for and prepared family dinners. She enjoyed that, and so did her parents! We didn't count calories—we worked on self-image and health. She wanted to have kids someday but hadn't had her period for two years. She also wanted to run on the high school track team, but we agreed she'd only try out if her period came back first. That was her motivation and goal to reach for. We talked about self-image and the pressures of being a teenage girl. My girls, at the time, were similar in age.

Taylor was looking for fulfillment in self-image and having control over something in her life. She wanted to feel she was worth something, that she was enough. We worked on renewing her mind to think about the truth rather than self-demeaning thoughts.

- Do not conform to the pattern of this world but be transformed by the renewing of your mind. Then you will be able to test and approve what God's will is—his good, pleasing and perfect will (Rom. 12:2).
- Or do you not know that your body is a temple of the Holy Spirit within you, whom you have from God? You are not your own, for you were bought with a price. So glorify God in your body (I Cor. 6:19–20 ESV).

Taylor began menstruating again the day after track tryouts. We celebrated with shouts and all kinds of jumping! She talked to the coach, had a private tryout, and made the team. This beautiful, hurting teenager was literally being eaten alive by Satan's lies she couldn't get out of her head. The truth is, God created her perfectly beautiful in his image. She didn't grow up knowing that. But once she saw the beauty of God, she reflected his truths through her image, radiating light and joy, allowing God to fill her. She learned food was not the enemy, Satan was.

TRICKY, TRICKY

We try to fill ourselves with things that don't fulfill. Food never fulfills—the lack of it or the overabundance of it.

How many *natural* foods can you name that are fatty, sugary, and salty all at the same time? Can you think of any? Using the combination of fat, salt, and sugar is how the food industry gets us to eat and buy more food.[36] They trick our bodies into wanting more by combining these ingredients that weren't naturally created together for a reason. And then we get addicted—I mean real addiction akin to drug addiction. We need to have more to satisfy our insatiable craving, and suddenly, we don't know how to have leftovers. An open package of cookies needs to be finished off because we have another Texas-sized Costco package calling out our name from inside the pantry. We reason, "I already blew it, so why not polish off the bag?"

On either side of being under- or overweight is the desire for control. We want to control (anorexia) or *not* have self-control (overeating) of what we put into our bodies. The question is why? There is an underlying pain that needs to be addressed. Self-worth. In my experience, when we strip away excuses, self-worth is the number one reason clients come in for nutrition counseling. They don't feel they are good enough, that they have worth. They may not know, or have forgotten, that God knit them beautifully and with purpose while they were in their mother's womb (Ps. 139:13–16). Food is not the enemy, Satan's lies are. "When he [Satan] lies, he speaks his native language, for he is a liar and the father of lies" (John 8:44).

LOSE THE ADDICTION

When we eat food in its most natural form in balanced proportions, we typically lose weight and lose our addiction(s). God built into our bodies a natural nutrition plan, but we want something different than what he made. We want to eat sweet, crunchy, salty, and fatty foods for comfort, but when our pants get tighter, our comfort foods don't feel so comfortable anymore. Our tongues look to satisfy our addictions, and we salivate until it's rewarded. But God also took care of that. Our tongues change according to what we feed them, desiring more of what we eat. We must make *conscious* decisions to change what we put into our mouths so we desire healthier foods. I am currently fasting from dark chocolate because once a week became once a day, became twice a day, became out of control. The less I have it, the less I desire it. This mechanism is also handily built into our bodies.

I always ask my clients, "What are the top three things you know you need to change in your eating habits?" I almost always hear, "I eat too much sugar." We are sugar addicts, and it's not funny. We joke saying, "I'm addicted to sugar," but not when we say, "I'm addicted to opioids." But what you may not realize is that you are in a very similar battle. Addiction is hard to break no matter the addiction: pornography, alcohol, gambling, drugs, sugar. It is serious. In the Bible, food addiction has a name: "gluttony" (Prov. 23:2). Gluttony is a sin that needs to be repented of and creates suffering in many lives. It is a genuine battle. Gluttony is difficult to repent of, and much guilt and shame circle around you if you struggle with this, but like with other sufferings, there is hope because God can change us with his power. He truly can. Go to the *Study Guide for Beauty Beyond the Thorns* to work through this section to begin your personal journey toward fulfillment.

MORE THAN CONQUERERS

God gives us the strength to overcome, but first, we must recognize our fulfillment comes from him and nothing else. Only he is the heart-shaped peg that fits into our heartfelt need. Sugar will not fulfill us. I've seen many clients find hope, drop weight, and become fulfilled once they understand that fulfillment comes from God, not from appearance. Eat what he has provided naturally for you. That's what Daniel did. "Daniel resolved not to defile himself with the royal food and wine, and he asked the chief official for permission not to defile himself in this way" (Dan. 1:8). For ten days, Daniel and his friends ate only vegetables and drank only water. "At the end of the ten days, they looked healthier and better nourished than any of the young men who ate the royal food." None of the other men who were being considered to enter the King's service equaled Daniel and his friends' health and wisdom, so they were chosen (Dan. 1:11–19).

Now I'm not saying everyone should go vegetarian. You can if you want, but what I *am* saying is don't go "royal." We don't need to eat portion sizes as big as Texas. We can make conscious decisions instead of eating mindlessly, especially while eating out.

We are addicted to food, and yet we cry out to God wondering why we can't lose weight. This too is a spiritual battle, folks. Satan doesn't want you to like yourself or find worth. True worth isn't found in appearance. We can only find it by believing how God feels about us. In him is where we find our *true* identity.

So God created man in his own image, in the image of God he created him; male and female he created them (Gen. 1:27).

Food is not the only thing we get addicted to. Addictions are prevalent in society, but we can overcome and find fulfillment in him rather than in addiction.

GOODBYE TO ALCOHOL

I received a letter from a man who has struggled with alcohol addiction for fifteen years. He wrote a goodbye letter to alcohol at the beginning of his sobriety journey. He is learning to receive love from God and find his way through addiction with help from a power greater than himself. I'm so thankful he shared this letter with me and gave me permission to share it with you.

Dear Alcohol,

We have been hanging out with each other for over 15 years now, and what a rollercoaster ride it has been. I was initially warned about what would happen if I spent too much time with you, but what did my parents or anyone else know? As any other stubborn teenager would do, I did exactly what I was told not to do, and man did it feel good! You assured me that nothing would go wrong and "what mom and dad didn't know wouldn't hurt them." No matter the circumstance, you would be there to celebrate with me when I was riding high and pick me back up off the ground when I was feeling down and out. You were right about one thing. You were always there.

For a while there, with the help of some of my other friends, I thought we were getting away with anything we wanted, and it was our little secret. How naïve I was to believe that that was the truth. Through the last year of high school, college years and every year of my adult life since then, I can honestly say we have probably had a closer relationship than any other I've had. Regardless of who knew how much time we were spending together while in another relationship or on my own, I didn't care because you always made me feel exactly the way I wanted to. You made me happy, comfortable, confident. At least you did for a while.

As time went on and I started hanging out more with other friends or family, working long hours during the day, going to events on the weekends, you began to get jealous that I wasn't including you in everything. Eventually you convinced me that you could be around, and we could be in control of ourselves when we had to take things seriously. Again, how naïve I was. I risked a lot of time, money, my reputation, and even my life to have you around, but the time has come to make a change.

For over 15 years you have been in control, the power over me in my life and the thing I have always turned to and relied on. I can truly now say that I have found a power greater than you and greater than myself that I can rely on and ask for help and support whenever I need. That power was and has been there all my life, but I was too blind to bring it into focus. For that I have to take the blame and accept that I have made some wrong decisions, but at least now I am comfortable doing so. I blame myself for deciding to drink but blame you for taking over my mind and body to make decisions, doing and saying things that I otherwise would not have. The power I was just alluding to is God. God has spoken to me and has assured me that there is a plan for me, a plan that will allow me to be eternally grateful and happy. One that I can take what I have experienced and learned and use it to help not only myself, but others who are seeking that greater power. This plan does not involve you [alcohol].

In most circumstances, the saying goes that the hardest thing to do in life is to say goodbye. Because of you, I have had to do it more times than I am proud of and would like to admit. And yes, it was hard. Goodbye to relationships, goodbye to playing soccer competitively, to good health, to memories, goodbye to previous jobs. It seems like goodbye has become a normalcy in my life for over 15 years now, and it is because of you. In this circumstance, the goodbye will not be hard. This goodbye is to you. I will have no regrets or wishes in the future to come back to this moment to do things differently or prevent it.

Goodbye alcohol and may you never return or make me have to say goodbye to anything or anyone else because of you ever again. Goodbye.

LIFE THROUGH THE SPIRIT—ROMANS 8

Please grab a Bible or Bible app and read all of Romans chapter 8. Every single word is so helpful to read here. Some highlights:

- Therefore, there is now no condemnation for those who are in Christ Jesus ...
- Those who live according to the flesh have their minds set on what the flesh desires; but those who live in accordance with the Spirit have their minds set on what the Spirit desires.
- For if you live according to the flesh, you will die; but if by the Spirit you put to death the misdeeds of the body, you will live.
- For those who are led by the Spirit of God are the children of God. The Spirit you received does not make you slaves, so that you live in fear again; rather, the Spirit you received brought about your adoption to sonship. And by him we cry, "*Abba,* Father." The Spirit himself testifies with our spirit that we are God's children. Now if we are children, then we are heirs—heirs of God and co-heirs with Christ, if indeed we share in his sufferings in order that we may also share in his glory.
- I consider that our present sufferings are not worth comparing with the glory that will be revealed in us.
- Who shall separate us from the love of Christ? Shall trouble or hardship or persecution or famine or nakedness or danger or sword?

WHO YOU ARE IN HIM BRINGS TRUE FULFILLMENT

Satan and his minion demons try to separate us from God. But don't let them. Fight them with the truth about who and whose you are. Instead of food and other addictions, God's Word can be our go-to comfort. There will be a feast one day that will equal no other when we get to heaven. Yes, we will feast in heaven, but probably not on Reddi-wip. In the meantime, remember this: Pain isn't meant for us to suffer, it's to help us grow stronger. Pain provides the resistance we need to grow. Sometimes it's hard, and it hurts to accept love. Some of us have an easier time giving love than receiving it. Now is the time to receive the love your Father has for you. True *ful*fillment comes from who you are in him, not from your appearance or addictions. He always provides what we need. Only God can *ful*fill.

CHAPTER 17

The Gift of Provision – Exponential Multiplication

How can we not know what provision is when God made creation to reproduce fish, fowl, beasts, plants, and trees?

FISH FIGHT

I love getting into fish fights! When I win, that is. There's nothing like casting my line into the river's still pools and waiting for that expectant bite. What a feeling to reel in the catch!

One fish fight may hook you. It was a battle several years ago between me and a leviathan-sized trout from the waters of the Arkansas River. Long, juicy night crawlers were the usual bait of choice. I had been scoring bites all morning, but I could not seem to hook and seal a deal. Mark was upstream, not exactly getting any contracts signed either.

Finally, a tug—a *big* one! I pull and jerk quickly to hook him, then pull and reel, pull and reel as fast as I can. But I'm losing tension. I feel the fight of the fish floundering under the river current. I can't lose tension, or we lose our dinner! Instinctively, I grab the line, drop the pole, and begin pulling the line with both hands. As the filament line piles in a coil next to me, I cry out to Mark, *"I caught a big one!"* I continue pulling in the line with both hands while said husband rushes toward me, watching in disbelief—not at the fish, but at me. I guess he's never seen anyone fish in this manner without a pole.

We watch the slippery, red trout flap wildly at the end of the line as he skims across the sparkling, sunlit waters and onto the river embankment. Mark could land some rather good bait himself with how far his jaw drops. He looks up at me, and together we cheer. We get to eat trout tonight!

Catching one fish took a half day's work and fed one man and one woman. I know of a man who created thousands of fish instantaneously to feed five thousand men, plus women and children, as much fish and bread as they wanted. This man's name was Jesus. The feeding of the 5,000+ is the only miracle, besides Jesus' resurrection from the dead, recorded in all four Gospels.

THE HEALINGS AT THE FEEDING OF THE 5,000+

The first enormous meal was provided for the Jewish crowd near the Sea of Galilee in Bethsaida (Matt. 14:13–21). Jesus had gone there initially to mourn because he was grieving the murder of his cousin John the Baptist. But like paparazzi find celebrities, crowds of people found Jesus. They gathered in this area from surrounding villages, having walked for many miles.

Despite Jesus' personal pain, he didn't turn people away. Instead, he responded to them with deep compassion and healed *their* hurts. By evening, the disciples thought Jesus should send everyone home to eat. They hadn't eaten all day. Jesus said to the disciples, "They do not need to go away. *You* give them something to eat" (Matt. 14:16). They heard this impossible task and answered, but "We have here only five loaves of bread and two fish," (v. 17) and "Eight months' wages would not buy enough bread for each one to have a bite!" (John 6:7).

Dumbfounded, the disciples looked at one another, scratching their heads. Jesus stepped forward and motioned for the people to come closer and sit in groups on the grass. He took the fish and loaves of bread, looked toward heaven, gave thanks, then broke the loaves, handing them to the disciples. Suddenly, unexpectedly, and instantaneously, the five loaves of bread multiplied to ten! To twenty! To two hundred! To two thousand! Enough to satiate the appetites of *up to 20,000* people.[37] Mathematicians and scientists had never seen anything multiply and divide so rapidly. It simply didn't add up! Each person ate and had their fill. Afterward, the twelve disciples collected twelve basketfuls of leftover food. A lesson for the twelve, and for us. Jesus provided more than enough.

THE HEALINGS AT THE FEEDING OF THE 4,000+

On another occasion, Jesus fed a hungry crowd of four thousand Gentile men, plus women and children (Matt. 15:32–39). Jesus was walking along the south side of the Sea of Galilee near the Decapolis and went up on a mountainside. Again, crowds followed him and brought their sick family members and friends, and Jesus healed them. The mute now spoke. The lame walked. The blind could see. These healings occurred over three days. "Jesus called his disciples to him and said, 'I have compassion for these people; they have already been with me three days and have nothing to eat. I do not want to send them away hungry, or they may collapse on the way'" (v. 32).

Even though the disciples witnessed the last miraculous mass feeding—and collected leftovers—they again asked Jesus where they could possibly get enough food in that remote area to feed the multitudes. They didn't remember the basketfuls of leftover food from the previous multiplication miracle. Oh, how easily we forget the power of God. God still feeds the multitudes. He creates and multiplies fish in the waters, beasts on the ground, seeds of the earth, and birds in the sky.

GOD STILL CARES FOR THE MULTITUDES

To give you a visual of how many people were at these enormous assemblies, imagine a large city arena like the Pepsi Center in Denver, capacity 18,007. People have come from all over to see Jesus, hear his teachings, and be healed of their diseases. When Jesus sees the people coming toward him, and observes their needs, again he wells up with compassion and gushes over with love. One by one, he heals the lame, the blind, the deaf, the emotionally tormented. He interacts personally with each sick person and his/her family to learn of each ailment so he can heal them. Instant, miraculous healings are taking place. Everyone is astounded. For the first time, their loved one can see! Canes and assistive devices are chucked far, far away! The deaf can hear themselves giving thanks and praise to God! Laughter, amazement, dancing, and joyful expressions come from those who their Healer has already touched. Hope, faith, and tremendous anticipation burst from those waiting their turn. And then Jesus feeds them.

Jesus is still with us and is filled with compassion, wanting one-on-one interactions with us. He wants to listen to our needs and heal our hurts. He is always available, and we don't have to travel to reach him. He is as close to you as your soul. His Spirit surrounds you. God provides for our needs daily. Like his disciples were expected and taught to figure out a way to help meet the needs of the hungry, we too are given the task of helping those who need a hand. We are called to compassion—to notice needs around us and respond in love. God will miraculously multiply our efforts to make a difference in ways we cannot even see. He multiplied the little boy's lunch his mother loving prepared for him that day. No matter how small your gift, you never know the effect it can have on one individual or even on the masses.

Miracles never cease. God performs them daily, and they are still nothing less than miraculous. Like he gave the disciples bread to feed the hungry crowds, he gives us the responsibility to take care of those around us. God provides us with resources, and he will multiply our efforts, but we must take the step of giving before he can multiply. Who is it that needs a hand around you? Who is God asking you to provide bread for? There will be leftovers. Giving begets giving. "The LORD is my shepherd, I lack nothing" (Ps. 23:1).

CHAPTER 18

The Gift of a Shepherd – Jesus Rescues Cast Sheep

How can we understand the gift of our Shepherd
if we don't understand the needs of a sheep?

WOMAN BENT DOUBLE

There is a healing story in the Bible of a woman bent double (Luke 13:10–17). She probably had ankylosing spondylitis—arthritic inflammation and excessive curvature of the spine. There is no cure.[38] The affliction of the woman, it appears from Scripture, was due to Satan's bondage. The woman bent double had been in this condition for eighteen years when Jesus noticed her at the synagogue. Of course, this healing happened on the Sabbath, much to the religious leaders' chagrin.

"Come to me," Jesus said as he saw her, "'you are set free from your infirmity.' Then he put his hands on her, and immediately she straightened up and praised God" (Luke 13:12-13). When Jesus asked the woman, who couldn't look up, to go to him, she bumbled her way toward the direction of his voice. And when she reached him ...

Boom! Jesus saw, had compassion, touched, and healed. After eighteen years of walking with her spine at a 90° angle like an

L-square, she was instantly straightened by Jesus. Do you know what happened next? It was the Sabbath, so it's predictable: The synagogue ruler *didn't* see, *didn't* have compassion, *didn't* touch, and *didn't* heal. Instead, he got mad. What the heck? How could someone be so spineless and not rejoice that the bent double woman was standing upright? He was completely blind and bent double to the fact this woman was standing up straight as a yardstick! He was like an L-square facing the ground. I don't suspect he would have followed Jesus' voice. But we can. His voice is right there in the red words in the Gospels of Matthew, Mark, Luke, and John. We can go to him there any day of the week.

Jesus called out the synagogue ruler and the other religious leaders, "You hypocrites! Doesn't each of you on the Sabbath untie your ox or donkey from the stall and lead it out to give it water? Then should not this woman, a daughter of Abraham, whom Satan has kept bound for eighteen long years, be set free on the Sabbath day from what bound her?" (Luke 13:15–16).

Good question. "When he said this, all his opponents were humiliated, but the people were delighted with all the wonderful things he was doing" (Luke 13:17).

SEE

We must see people. We must be compassionate. We must reach out and touch others; our efforts will help heal something in those people. We are all bent double in some way: out of touch, out of whack, burned out, checked out, out of order, out of tune, out to lunch, or out of line.

We must reach out, look out, figure out, and not miss out on the lessons of healing and joy we can learn from this story. This woman was in the right place at the right time. She didn't approach Jesus; she may not have known he was there. How could she see anything but the pebbles and cracks in stone pavement below her feet?

But she—she caught *his* eye. He saw her and didn't look away. He zoomed in on her and conquered Satan by restoring this woman's physical and emotional well-being.

This is a sign of what was and is to come for each of us, no matter our type of suffering. Jesus sees each of us. He wants us to "come" to be healed of our infirmity, our binding. He is waiting to look us in the eye, face to face, and say, "You are set free from your infirmity." This will happen when he returns to take us home if we respond to him in this life differently than the Pharisees and other religious leaders did.

The woman bent double had no choice but to face the ground for eighteen years. You may be feeling low too. Let Jesus lift your chin and look into your eyes. He is with you right now, and he sees you. You can look to the Shepherd, who has a purpose for your life and wants to lead you to green pastures and cool brooks. Sadly, if we don't choose to follow him, our default mode is to follow sin and Satan. It's just easier because we have a sinful nature.

THE GREAT SHEPHERD

I am the good shepherd; I know my sheep and my sheep know me—just as the Father knows me and I know the Father—and I lay down my life for the sheep (John 10:14–15).

Philip W. Keller, author and former shepherd, writes in his book, *A Shepherd Looks at Psalm 23*, about the characteristics of sheep and their dependence on their shepherd. According to Keller, nothing calms and comforts sheep more than the presence of their shepherd. Sheep tend to be skittish and need more careful supervision than any other type of livestock. They are completely dependent on their caretaker to protect them from all that endangers or disturbs. We, like sheep, tend to go astray, and there is nothing that can quiet our fears and troubles more than the presence of our Shepherd.[39] "I will fear no evil, for you are with me" (Ps. 23:4).

Placing your faith in Jesus, whom you can't physically see, may be the most challenging thing you will ever do in life, but it is the most critical decision you can make. If you've been delaying seeing him, stop reading this book and open your Bible to Matthew or John and begin reading. You will find his voice in the red print. When you meet him there, let yourself go to him like the woman bent double was called to come. Follow him—the Great Shepherd of your soul.

CAST SHEEP

When a sheep looks for a comfortable place to rest, such as a soft, rounded hollow in the ground, and lies down there, he can easily become cast on his back, unable to get to his feet. If stuck there for longer than twenty-four hours, he will die. The shepherd must continually watch his flock to protect them from danger—in this case, a comfortable place.[40]

"There is the Shepherd's deep concern; his agonizing search; his longing to find the missing one; his delight in restoring it not only to its feet but also to the flock as well as to himself."[41] Jesus spots us in our troubles and rescues us in ways we don't even know the half about. We are precious in his sight. He is our Good Shepherd. He restores my soul.

> The Lord is my shepherd, I lack nothing.
> He makes me lie down in green pastures,
> he leads me beside quiet waters,
> he refreshes my soul.
> He guides me along the right paths
> for his name's sake.
> Even though I walk
> through the darkest valley,

I will fear no evil,
   for you are with me;
your rod and your staff,
   they comfort me.
You prepare a table before me
   in the presence of my enemies.
You anoint my head with oil;
   my cup overflows.
Surely your goodness and love will follow me
   all the days of my life,
and I will dwell in the house of the LORD
   forever (Psalm 23:1–6).

CHAPTER 19

The Gift of Touch – Lepers

How can we understand the value of touch if we've never held the hand of a sufferer?

LEPROSY

In the Gospels, Jesus healed various lepers. There was no cure for leprosy in the first century. It's a disease that starts small but increasingly damages the body over time. Leprosy is symbolic of how our sin begins small but spreads, leading to other sins which cause damage to others and our relationship with God. "A man with leprosy came to him and begged him on his knees, 'If you are willing, you can make me clean. 'Jesus reached out his hand and touched the man. 'I am willing,' he said. 'Be clean!' Immediately, the leprosy left him, and he was cleansed" (Mark 1:40–42).

Jesus urged the man to go directly to the priest, who would provide him with a ritual certification of cleansing, then pronounce him ceremonially clean. This certification would allow the healed man reinstatement into society. He was then to offer ritualistic sacrifices. Jesus respected the law by warning the man to go to the priest before telling anyone of his healing. Because the man did not, Jesus had to stay on the periphery of town due to the rise in adversaries who wanted him killed. Yet people still came to him. The healing of lepers was a testimony to the divine power of Jesus since Jews believed only God could cure leprosy.

Like menstruating women and other outcasts, lepers were "unclean" and were not to be touched, mingle in society, go to the market, or worship in the synagogue. I find it ironic that Jesus didn't have to touch lepers to heal them, yet he did. His perfect love and compassion touched them because he wanted to initiate their emotional healing, not just their physical recovery. They were "unclean" to society, but to Jesus, they were human beings that his Father had created. He communicated his love for them with deep compassion and showed the crowds they were valuable by extending his hand and touching them.

Who could use a touch from you? A lonely elderly person in a nursing home? A baby left in a playpen? A lonely teen who feels rejected by his/her peers? A single parent? Many people today feel untouchable, unworthy of love. But everyone is worthy of touch. Touch heals. Imagine how the "unclean" felt when touched for the first time in perhaps many years. Healthy touch signifies love and acceptance. Without it, our lives deteriorate. With it, our lives are invigorated. To be denied touch is to be deprived of an essential need for human survival. To deny giving touch is to deny a gift God gives you to extend to others.

BANDON, THAILAND – April 8, 1979

I saw absolutely the most hideous beggar on earth today on the train just before we crossed the border into Thailand. This dude came walking into my carriage not long after the train stopped, and I swear if I had been ten years younger, he would have given me nightmares for months. His body seemed okay, but it was his face that gave me the shakes—his entire nose had rotted away, so much that I could see his sinuses through the

hole, and his lips were fused together except for a small gap through which he was attempting to sing. I couldn't bear to look at him when he came to me, I just prayed he'd go away. Jesus, the things some people in this world have to live with.
– Mark Anderson Steiner, age 19

My husband took a year off from college to travel the world, spending many months in Thailand. There he saw a leper and the grotesque effects this disease has on the human body. I find it interesting that Mark wrote in his travel journal, "I just prayed he'd go away." This is not the Mark I know today, who is the most compassionate man I have known. Mark didn't have a relationship with God in 1979 when he saw the leprous man. He was prompted to pray not for the leper but *for his* comfort—for the man to go away.

SCIENTIFIC DESCRIPTION OF LEPROSY

The Centers for Disease Control describes "Hansen's disease (also known as leprosy) [as] an infection caused by slow-growing bacteria called *Mycobacterium leprae*. It can affect the nerves, skin, eyes, and lining of the nose (nasal mucosa). With early diagnosis and treatment, the disease can be cured."[42] The following subsection is an explanation by author Alan L. Gillen from his book, *The Genesis of Germs:*

Like leprosy, sin starts out small but can then spread, leading to other sins in causing great damage in our relationship with God and others. Studying leprosy helps us see why pain is a valuable "gift," a survival mechanism to warn us of danger in this cursed world. Without pain and suffering, we might be like lepers, unable to recognize that something is terribly wrong and that we need the healing touch of God. As Dr. Brand (the late world-renowned orthopedic surgeon and leprosy physician) said, I cannot think of a greater gift that I could give my leprosy patients than pain.[43]

Pain is a warning signal. It is a gift. We would know so if we had leprosy.

GOD CANNOT BE BOUGHT

Written around 550 BC, in the book of 2 Kings, is a story of a valiant soldier, commander of the army of the king of Aram, who had leprosy. Naaman's wife knew about a prophet in Samaria who could cure him of his leprosy. After receiving permission from the king of Aram, Naaman packed gold, silver, ten sets of clothing and went on his way. When the king of Israel read the letter from the king of Aram requesting healing for Naaman, he tore his robes and said, "Am I God?" (2 Kings 5:7). He knew only God could heal. Elisha, the prophet of God, heard that the king tore his robes and said, "Have the man come to me and he will know that there is a prophet in Israel" (v. 8). So Naaman went to his door and Elisha sent a messenger to him saying, "Go, wash yourself seven times in the Jordan, and your flesh will be restored, and you will be cleansed" (v. 10).

If I had leprosy and one of God's prophets told me the prescription for healing, I would hope I would follow his protocol. But Naaman had in mind a particular way he thought Elisha should heal him—by waving his hand magically over him and having him wash in cleaner water than the muddy waters of the Jordan River. He said, "Couldn't I wash in them [rivers of Damascus] and be cleansed?" (v. 12). Then he went off in a rage. I guess he was used to calling the shots as commander of an army.

However, Naaman's servants persuaded him to do exactly what Elisha had told him (smart servants). So, he dipped himself in the Jordan seven times "... and his flesh was restored and became clean like that of a young boy." Naaman went back to the man of God, stood before him, and said, "Now I know that there is no God in all the world except in Israel. So please accept a gift from your servant" (vv. 14–15). But Elisha refused to accept anything and told him to go in peace.

The number seven has significance because it is a symbol of completeness. Bathing in the Jordan shows it was not the water's cleanness that healed him; it was God.[44]

Naaman headed for home, but suddenly, Gehazi, a servant of Elisha, ran toward the chariot. When he caught up, Naaman jumped down to make sure everything was okay. Gehazi lied through his teeth, saying his master Elisha sent him to ask for a talent of silver and two sets of clothing. Gehazi wanted to be paid some bank for the healing. Naaman gladly gave him two talents of silver and two sets of clothing. When Gehazi returned home, he put the gifts in the house, and Elisha asked, "Where have you been Gehazi?"

"Your servant didn't go anywhere," Gehazi lied again.

But Elisha said to him, "'Was not my spirit with you when the man got down from his chariot to meet you? Is this the time to take money or to accept clothes …? Naaman's leprosy will cling to you and to your descendants forever.' Then Gehazi went from Elisha's presence and his skin was leprous—it had become as white as snow" (vv. 21–26).

Some reflection on Naaman's cleansing story: Healing (representative of grace) from the divine God cannot be bought. And it will not be given in the way we think it should be given. When Naaman finally obeyed God's prophet, he was healed. He received the gift of God's grace. How many times do we miss out on a blessing of God because we don't want to do something the way God instructs? Naaman expected some kind of magic show with waving of hands and cleansing in clean waters. But obedience is one of God's requirements to receive his gifts, *whether or not* the request makes sense to us. The worldly wealth that Gehazi desired defiled the grace of God.

We cannot buy God, which is why Elisha refused the generous gifts Naaman brought. Elisha did not seek monetary gain for proclaiming the word of the Lord. Divine grace healed Naaman, not Elisha. Gehazi not only lied to Elisha but to Naaman as well. His greed and deceitfulness (disobedience) earned him the high-priced consequence of a lifetime of leprosy: a harsh lesson—one that would be recorded in the Bible to communicate God's seriousness that grace is given as a gift. There are consequences we suffer when we defile the grace of God.

TOUCH WITH LOVE

Many of us have given up reaching out in faith to "touch" Jesus. Instead, we are waiting for Jesus to "touch" us. When we feel he hasn't, we claim he is non-existent or doesn't care. We have a choice: Do we turn toward God in trust, or do we turn away from him in bitterness? Will we remain bitter and angry, or let God reveal himself and his beauty beyond the thorns to us throughout our suffering? Who are some metaphorical lepers around you that could use a touch? Maybe God wants to heal a pain they have through you.

CHAPTER 20

The Gift of Gratitude – One Leper

If we don't express gratitude, is it because we feel entitled?

TEN LEPERS

Luke's Gospel tells a story of ten lepers who cried out to Jesus as they traveled to Jerusalem, "Jesus, Master, have pity on us!" Jesus replied to them, "Go show yourselves to the priests." Miraculously, he healed all ten while they went on their way.

> One of them, when he saw he was cured, came back, praising God in a loud voice. He threw himself at Jesus' feet and thanked him—and he was a Samaritan. Jesus asked, "Were not all ten cleansed? Where are the other nine? Has no one returned to give praise to God except this foreigner?" Then he said to him, "Rise and go; your faith has made you well" (Luke 17:15–19).

Our first response may be to react in disbelief at the incomprehensible ingratitude and apparent entitlement of the nine who offered no thanks for being healed from leprosy. Instead of reflecting on the nine who were ungrateful, let's focus on the one who found Jesus and expressed his gratitude. When we look at our lives, how often do *we* forget to be grateful for the many things God does for us in a day? Is it nine times out of ten?

This Gentile's response was to *find* Jesus, *thank* him, *throw* himself at his feet, and *praise* him in a *loud* voice. What else could he have done to express his gratitude? How does your appreciation of God measure up? His gratitude resulted in joyful praise. He didn't hold back his expression because he knew it was God Almighty who had healed him.

Are we so used to God doing things for us we take him for granted? Afflictions in my life have deepened my gratitude for things and people I used to take for granted. Think about a wound you have had in your life, like a skinned knee. God formed new skin cells and healed that wound. Isn't that remarkable? I mean, I can't make new skin cells. Can you? Oh, how often we take our Healer for granted. When God does something nice for us, let there be no mistake in his mind of how grateful we are for his mighty workings in our lives! Let us find him, thank him, bow at his feet, and joyfully praise him with gratitude.

> Praise the LORD, my soul,
>   and forget not all his benefits—
> who forgives all your sins
>   and heals all your diseases,
> who redeems your life from the pit
>   and crowns you with love and compassion,
> who satisfies your desires with good things
>   so that your youth is renewed like the eagles (Ps. 103:2–5).

NORMAL

A beautiful gift born from suffering is gratitude. Or rather it *can be*. Sometimes in my life, now being one of them, I have longed to do "normal" things—things like clean the dishes, vacuum, drive, walk, visit someone, or pick up the dog doo. After my first disability, when I began walking again, it was a glorious experience for me to walk around the grass and pick up the dog doo. No kidding. And as I was doing it, I was praising God by singing! The neighbors were like, "If that makes you so happy, wanna come over here next?" If they had really asked, I would have! Most people dread this task. But I can tell you outright: I long for the ability to pick up the dog doo again.

When abilities or things become unavailable to us, we don't take them for granted as much. It is a gift to have the ability to walk and drive and do chores. Remember when you begrudgingly do a chore or an undesirable task, that others *long* to do these things. We have so much to be grateful for, so let's get to it and let God know how much we appreciate him by finding him, bowing before him, and praising him in gratitude for all he has done and for the abilities he has given us. Let us strive to thank him ten out of ten times for all he does to take care of us. Thanks is better when it is given, spoken, expressed. Don't forget to say it and pray it!

CHAPTER 21

The Gift of a Good Samaritan – Inconvenient Love

How can we know how to be a Good Samaritan if we don't allow ourselves to be inconvenienced to help someone in need?

BARB

My friend Barb is a divine gift—a Good Samaritan. From the first day we met in early 2019, she has ministered to me, intravenously feeding me liquid love. I met Barb when she and my friend Jen, her daughter-in-law, came to visit me. They heard about my grievous pain and disability and wanted to provide some company and compassion. Barb came repeatedly, and each time her visits became longer. She cried with me over my health limitations and my dying father. My heart was breaking. I used to be a caretaker for my dad, and now I was also in need. I hadn't seen Dad in a month, and after I expressed my lament, Barb said, "Well, what if I take you?" It was an offer difficult to accept for several reasons:

1. Only Mark knew the details of how to get me down the ramp and into the car
2. It was a 45-minute drive to the assisted living facility

3. It was unpredictable how many hours we'd be there
4. Lunch was uncertain, even if we'd have time to eat

Barb agreed to all these things, picked me up, and spent count-less hours helping me to make the end of Dad's life more comfort-able. She made it easier on me by saying, "Now what day shall we plan for next? You let me know." This was so much easier than ask-ing her for yet another favor after she had already outdone herself. She offered herself repeatedly.

The first time Barb met Dad, he was writhing and moaning in his sleep. We cleaned his room, waiting for him to awaken. Even-tually, I tried shaking him, but he wasn't coming to. An ambulance came—Dad was reaching diabetic coma. If Barb hadn't taken me to see Dad that day, he would have died.

Twice a week, Barb picked me up to help Dad, stepping in like a daughter to lovingly care for him. She'd help wash his encrusted eyes, clean his glasses, buy him a Diet Coke, and hold the straw for him to sip. She cleaned his place, fed him, brought him jam, kissed his forehead, and consoled me through his death. Dad's face lit up when he saw her, and he signed one of his drawings and gave it to her as a gift of love and an expression of his appre-ciation.

A BOWL OF SOUP FOR DAD—August 27, 2019

Finally, hospice accepted him. My daddy can't speak but an occa-sional whisper. He tried to tell me something, but I couldn't un-derstand. I strained to hear as I placed my ear near his lips. A faint whisper, but so weak I couldn't understand. I tried and tried to hear, but I couldn't meet his needs if that is what he was trying to voice. My heart was aching. I didn't know what he needed.

One of three phrases I understood today:

- "I saw your mother today ..." (Mom died fourteen years ago.)
- "Ice cream ..."
- "Thank you," he faintly whispered to the CNA, who wiped his mouth with a warm washcloth after lunch.

I rubbed his back as I spoon-fed him broth from his chicken noodle soup, taking over for Barb. He only wants liquids now. Everything else requires too much effort. The bones in his shoulder blades and spine are what I rubbed through a paper-thin layer of skin. Where has my daddy gone? Piece by piece, he is disappearing. Every time I see him, a piece of his mind or his body has vanished. His voice is gone—I'm never to hear, "I love you so, so much!" ever again—an ever-present aspect of our times together or closing our phone conversations. His 180-pound body is now a scant 120. Where did it go? Will someone please tell me? How can he be disappearing so quickly? Eye contact—my favorite thing to do when I saw him was to lock eyes and smile at each other. Today he had one eye open, and one eye shut; both eyes shut; both eyes open but staring down, looking somewhere beyond the present. I caught a glimpse when I kissed his forehead; his left eye looked at me, and I knew he saw his "Red."

He understood today—his mind was not gone. He couldn't speak but answered questions nonverbally. "Are you hungry?" No response. "Peanut butter and jelly?" A shake. "Grilled cheese?" A shake. "Chicken noodle soup?" A nod! Chicken noodle soup it is. And it just so happens to be on today's lunch menu. A bowl of chicken noodle soup for Dad. I believe God did that. He gave Dad a nod and served it right up for everyone in the dining room.

After sipping a few spoonsful of broth, Dad tried to whisper. I pulled my ear close, and after a few attempts, I heard it ever so faintly, "ice cream." The white melted cream dribbled from his mouth, but he swallowed more of that than anything. He loves vanilla ice cream. Barb handed me napkin after napkin to catch the melted dribbles between bites. He was eating! Who cares if he has diabetes when his body is starving for calories? Then we tried the butter pecan protein shake with a straw. He sucked and sucked and sucked. Who knew Dad likes butter pecan flavor? A new discovery late in life. Lunch was a success. More calories in him, providing for him another day of life.

So, is this what we do? Help him eat more so he can live longer? But he's ready to go. He wants to "go home." Is it cruel to celebrate Dad's intake of calories by providing more sustenance when what he wants is to go? It's a confusing time. As I feed him, my wheelchair next to his, I lean my body underneath his hunched body to speak into his eyes, "I love you so much, you know that, right?" A slow but definite nod. "Jesus is waiting for you to give you a crown. You'll get to see Mom again soon. Don't give up on your faith. God is with you even though this is so, so hard. Thank you for your faith, Dad, it has helped me to have mine." He's in there. He can hear, and he can understand, he just can't speak.

I don't know when the last time is that I'll get to see him. It feels eerily close. Tears catch in my throat. You know those tears you hold back? They get stuck right there. I cannot speak, or I will lose it. I can't talk to anyone about today, so I write. My whole body grieves as he disappears increasingly, day by day. As God prepares to bring him home, my throat finally opens, allowing tears to flow, then sobs I've stuffed in there unleash as the dam breaks.

After time, my whimpers turn to tears of joy as I think about your desire to go home. When you get there, for a moment, you will still be speechless as Jesus lays a crown of faithful victory on your head. Then your voice will burst forth, completely uninhibited, as you proclaim in loud accord with the angels and saints, "Glory be to God!" Then God will lock eyes with yours and tell you,

"Well done, Roger, my good and faithful servant. Well done!" And I imagine he will kiss you on your forehead.

GOODBYE DAD

"Goodbye for now, Dad." I will see you again. I will hear your voice again, and I will lock eyes and smile together with you again. We will eat chicken noodle soup and ice cream and drink butter pecan flavored protein shakes and laugh and talk and visit Harvey Park and enjoy another soda under the trees' shade. You will be okay. This will be okay. It feels you are moving piece by piece to the other side. "I love you so, so much, my sweet Dad. Goodbye for now."

Dad died two days later, on August 29, 2019. I never heard another word spoken by him. He never ate another meal. He closed his eyes and became unresponsive over the next two days. Most of us got to say our goodbyes throughout the day he died. I'm pretty sure he felt our kisses, my last near his right eye.

His final visitors came that evening. When the nurse went into his room to turn him, he awoke. She told him his granddaughter Jenny was there to see him. Nurse Sheila said he smiled a great big smile, and he was happier at that moment than she'd seen him during the three weeks he was at the 24-hour-care facility. My daughter Jenny and son-in-law Stephen ushered him into heaven with prayer and Scripture readings from Ps. 23, 2 Cor. 5, and 1 Cor. 15:50–58. "Where, O death, is your victory? Where, O death, is your sting?" He opened his right eye in response, and Jen called me so I got to say one more "I love you so, so much, Dad!" over speakerphone. Ten minutes later, after Jen and Stephen had left, Dad let go.

The battle has been won! Dad's battle scars have been transformed into a glorious new body, and he is wearing a heavenly crown. He is okay now. Everything is going to be okay.

Barb knew Dad for only a couple of months, but her love for him will last me a lifetime. This divinely given Good Samaritan ministered to him and to me. Without Barb I wouldn't have been able to help Dad as often through his last months. Barb continues to minister mercy, love, and care to me and my family. She let herself be inconvenienced and took time to love and care for Dad and me. What an example she has set for us of what a good neighbor embodies.

Not only did Barb help Dad and me spend time together during his last months, but her actions were used by God to help answer a prayer that had been looming in my heart for thirty years.

CHAPTER 22

The Gift of Forgiveness – A Thirty Year Prayer

How can we know what forgiveness is until we have been utterly broken by our sin?

DAD

I had been a Christian for a few years but struggled deeply to forgive Dad. When I was a kid, he was gruff. I didn't like to be around him. When there was a scramble to the dinner table, I'd make a flying leap for the chair farthest from him. Before bed, I knew I'd get in trouble if I didn't give him a peck on the cheek, so I mustered up the courage, then hit the hallway for bed like it was a slip-and-slide.

Dad was an elementary art teacher. For much of my childhood, he worked second and even third jobs to support his wife and five children. He was angry and stressed while at home. He never made one of my volleyball games that I can remember, but I remember every choir concert he attended because he always asked me, "Why don't you smile?" But I *was* smiling. I tried hard to please him, but he didn't notice my effort. With his feedback, I figured I sucked at singing.

One day, in my early twenties, I remember standing in a gift store trying to choose a birthday card for Dad. As I put each card back into its slot, I was heartbroken that the sentiments written in the cards were not truthful. I would not give him a card that said what I didn't feel. I decided then to try to have an open conversation with him about how we could grow in our relationship. I left his house with him saying, "Is our relationship really that bad?" We had a terrible relationship, and he thought it wasn't that bad?

I worked hard to strengthen our bond in my early twenties and took him out once a month for lunch. I didn't enjoy our times much because he talked mostly of himself. I still struggled with Dad, so I took my grief to God and fasted for my relationship with him—I needed help to forgive him. I couldn't find it within my power; I needed a superpower beyond my ability. I fasted for six days, drinking only water. I prayed, hoping God would change my heart so I could forgive Dad for all the pain he caused me, my siblings, and Mom.

As a young teenager, Dad hit me after I mowed our oversized lot to surprise him. I poured gasoline into the small tank of the lawnmower and oil into the even smaller one, just like he showed me. I finished the job in a couple of hours. My gift to him was thrown back in my face as his hand slapped my left cheek. "Do you see the oil and gas leaking together here?" he yelled as he pointed to the top of the mower. "You could have blown this thing up and killed yourself!" I shouted some retort back at him (surprising both of us), which garnered me my slap. I punished myself further by staying in bed for two days. Mom called the school to excuse me.

Then I ran away—to my best friend's house. I knew Mom and Dad would eventually find me there, so the next safest place I could think of was the elementary school park. I don't know how long I was there before my mom and siblings found me. I cried and begged Mom to leave him. Why wouldn't she leave him? All of us were afraid of him, including her. When we all walked back into the house a few hours later, Dad was sitting in the living room motionless, like petrified wood—or more like a petrified ghost. All color had drained from his face. I'd never seen *him* scared before. I actually felt pity for him. He brought all of this on himself, didn't he? Weekly counseling times were carved into his busy schedule. Dad had hit rock bottom.

HERMIT

When Mom died in 2007, Dad basically did too. He stayed in his home, hardly leaving for a decade. He kept Mom's room exactly as it had been—her sheets unchanged, a partially used water bottle on her nightstand, and folded towels in the laundry basket. The only thing that changed over the years was dust piling higher, hiding memories of what were once signs of her life.

One night in 2017, I received a call from a hospital that Dad had driven himself to their emergency room. He had blistering sores throughout the inside of his mouth and down his throat; he could hardly swallow. After brief observation, they sent him home. Not long after, he ended up at another hospital in the intensive care unit. He had been accidentally overdosing on his arthritis medication, which was causing the sores and additional life-threatening symptoms.

Dad almost died. He couldn't eat or drink because the sores hurt too much. He pulled out the feeding tube—he didn't like that thing at all. We fed him ice chips that sustained him for a bit, but as the days rolled by, his weight dropped. If he wouldn't eat or drink, or allow the feeding tube, he'd die.

A few years prior, I had developed a swallowing disorder after swallowing a large vitamin. For several months I had difficulty eating. Thankfully, I'm a nutritionist and had various ideas up my sleeve; the first, very thin baby food. While Dad was fighting for his life, I ran to the store.

Raspberry-pear baby food and a lot of prayers brought Dad out of the ICU. Once he was released, my siblings and I moved him into an assisted living facility and sold his precious home of 49 years. It was a sorrowful time, and believe you me, stressful.

Dad was helpless and had lost so much—not only his home and most of his belongings, but his independence as well. To help with his transition, his kids took turns eating a meal with him in the assisted living dining room. He had been a hermit for so long we wondered how he'd get along having to share each meal with others. He had no choice but to come out of the cave where he had been hiding.

I opted to be a caregiver for Dad and helped him three days a week. After two months, we had spent more time together than the entire decade before. Dad told me stories of his childhood, of being in the military, and of dating Mom. We ran errands together and placed his financial affairs in order. Finally, we looked forward to our times together.

TEARS

One day, Dad told me terrible memories of his childhood—how his father had tied him to a pole in the basement, whipped him with a belt, and then stomped on him. He told me about his aunt, who served him a raw chicken for dinner, while his cousins received a cooked chicken meal. He ran away as fast as he could. He told me he was made fun of at school because he stuttered. So he ran. Tears of pain flowed achingly from his eyes. His evident pain caused me to cry in disbelief at how certain family members had treated Dad during his childhood.

Compassion flowed from me, and a lot of things came together to help me forgive him. This conversation gave me insight as to why he was the way he was. I didn't recognize until then how much worse my life *could* have been—how much worse his life was than mine. I was thankful I was hit only once, but angry that his dad damaged this poor man in such a traumatic way. Who knows what my grandpa went through during his childhood? I grasped at that moment that I had had a dad all along, I just hadn't understood him. Now I understood that, although Dad was angry, he didn't beat us. He *stopped* that trend. I finally appreciated that Dad worked three jobs to provide for us and never served us a raw chicken dinner.

REALIZATION

I realized the missing piece, that not only did I need to forgive Dad, but that *I needed forgiveness from him*—for my hatred and judgment of him. I became utterly broken.

Understanding the circumstances in his life helped pivot me into that place of forgiveness. I learned that a prayer and fast thirty years prior was still ringing in the heart of God. He heard my prayer and orchestrated a time and a place to provide healing through forgiveness for both of us. That was the day my fast was answered. I was looking at the speck in his eye and not the plank in my own. I am convinced that's why it took me thirty years.

- Do not judge, or you too will be judged. For in the same way you judge others, you will be judged, and with the measure you use, it will be measured to you. Why do you look at the speck of sawdust in your brother's eye and pay no attention to the plank in your own eye? How can you say to your brother, "Let me take the speck out of your eye," when all the time there is a plank in your own eye? You hypocrite, first take the plank out of your own eye, and then you will see clearly to remove the speck from your brother's eye (Matt. 7:1–5).

HEALING

During the two-plus years Dad was at the assisted living facility, my heart healed further day by day. After that, I had no trouble choosing a birthday card for him. I even found a Superman one!

By the time Dad died, I felt at peace in our relationship. I finally felt adored by him—something I longed for my entire life. I finally felt warmth and love and personal interest. Dad also reached out to Mark and our girls more. Jen and Nicole got to know their grandfather better by spending time with him over peanut butter and jelly sandwiches and visits at the facility.

I am so grateful for the gift of forgiveness that God has given us. I now understand that forgiveness is a *gift*. I'm so glad Dad and I exchanged our gifts of forgiveness before it was too late. God gave me the desires of my heart, never forgetting my fast and prayer for restoration. God still heals. He heals hearts through forgiveness and provides restoration in relationships.

- So I turned to the Lord God and pleaded with him in prayer and petition, in fasting, and in sackcloth and ashes (Dan. 9:3).
- Be kind to one another, tenderhearted, forgiving one another, as God in Christ forgave you (Eph. 4:32).
- Be merciful, just as your Father is merciful. Do not judge, and you will not be judged. Do not condemn, and you will not be condemned. Forgive, and you will be forgiven. Give, and it will be given to you. A good measure, pressed down, shaken together and running over, will be poured into your lap. For with the measure you use, it will be measured to you (Luke 6:36–38).
- But when you fast, put oil on your head and wash your face, so that it will not be obvious to others that you are fasting, but only to your Father, who is unseen; and your Father, who sees what is done in secret, will reward you (Matt. 6:17–19).
- "Even now," declares the Lord, "return to me with all your heart, with fasting and weeping and mourning. Rend your heart and not your garments. Return to the LORD your God, for he is gracious and compassionate, slow to anger and abounding in love ..." (Joel 2:12–13).

- "Hear, LORD, and be merciful to me; LORD, be my help." You turned my wailing into dancing; you removed my sackcloth and clothed me with joy, that my heart may sing your praises and not be silent. LORD my God, I will praise you forever (Ps. 30:10–12).

CHAPTER 23

The Gift of Sight – The God Who Sees

*How can we know what sight is
without following the One who sees?*

SPOTLIGHT

I was recently lamenting to my friend Jen that often I don't feel seen when in my wheelchair. You'd think I'd stick out like a sore thumb in a crowd because of the wheelchair, but usually, the opposite is true. When I watch eyes pan the room, they often skip over me. I watch people act as if I'm not there.

My friend Jen wisely helped me see that all of us experience feeling unseen. We all feel others don't see us because either we're too young or too old; too intimidating or shy; single, married, divorced, or widowed; a teen or a child. Jen says in her book *Enough About Me*, "God made us to be light makers, and the spotlight is meant to shine right back on him."[45] I was thinking others should see me, instead of me trying to see them, reflecting God to them. Sometimes I forget the world doesn't revolve around me and others may be experiencing deeper pains than I am.

There is one who sees us perfectly—God. As we aim to become more like him, our vision sharpens, and we become more focused on others like he is, shining his light right back on him.

GOD SEES US WITH HIS EYES

- Does he who formed the *eye* not *see*? (Ps. 94:9).
- From heaven the Lord *looks* down and sees all mankind; from his dwelling place he *watches* all who live on earth (Ps. 33:13).
- For the *eyes* of the Lord range throughout the earth to strengthen those whose hearts are fully committed to him (2 Chron. 16:9).
- My help comes from the Lord, the Maker of heaven and earth. He will not let your foot slip–he who *watches* over you will not slumber; indeed, he who *watches* over Israel will neither slumber nor sleep. The Lord *watches* over you–the Lord is your shade at your right hand; the sun will not harm you by day, nor the moon by night. The Lord will keep you from all harm–he will *watch* over your life; the Lord will *watch* over your coming and going both now and forevermore (Ps. 121:2–8).

THE STORY OF HAGAR

In Genesis chapter 16, Sarai was having trouble believing God's promise that he would bless her and Abram with a son in their eighties. Sarai took God's promise into her own hands instead of trusting God to carry out his plan. She gave her maidservant Hagar to Abram to have relations and build their family through Hagar.

When Hagar learned of her pregnancy, she despised her mistress. Sarai mistreated Hagar, and Hagar ran away into the desert feeling hurt, abandoned, and unseen. As a poor, pregnant slave girl, alone in the desert, her future didn't look secure—if she survived the journey through the desert, she could not take care of herself or provide for her baby.

Here the story shifts: "The angel of the Lord found Hagar near a spring in the desert." He had good news, then bad news, then more good news. First, he told her, "... the Lord has heard of your misery." The bad news? She was to go back to Sarai and Abram. More good news—"[God] will so increase your descendants [through her baby Ishmael] that they will be too numerous to count."

The servant-concubine, Hagar, finally felt seen. She said to the angel of the Lord, "You are the God who sees me," and she gave him a new Hebrew name, El Roi, "The God who sees." Hagar felt seen by God in her distress, and it was only after she felt seen that she was strengthened to go back to her master and mistress to fulfill the Lord's plan. She now understood her purpose.

In Genesis 16:13, Hagar not only names God because she feels seen by him, but also because she now *sees him*—"'I have now seen the One who sees me.'" When we feel seen by God, our vision for others improves. It opens our eyes to realize, when in a room filled with people who don't see us, that they also feel unseen. We see what we haven't been seeing—or rather, *who* we haven't been see-ing—and can now extend compassion.

Praise be to the God and Father of our Lord Jesus Christ, the Father of compassion and the God of all comfort, who comforts us in all our troubles, so that we can comfort those in any trouble with the comfort we ourselves receive from God (2 Cor. 1:3–4).

Hagar received a glimpse of the Lord. We too have eyes to see—to receive a glimpse of God—by reading his truths. When we read and follow his Word, he changes us to become more like him. We can navigate our path better as he lights the way. We can walk into a crowded room with security knowing that someone—the One—sees us for who we are, and he loves us. And we can perceive others with eyes of compassion as God saw wandering Hagar.

GOD SEES YOU

God sees you too. He has a plan for your life. You are precious in his sight. You are his child, and he watches over you day and night. When you feel isolated in a crowded room, El Roi sees you. When you are alone, crying in your bed, El Roi sees you. When left out of a gathering and feeling alone and unseen, you are not. God is watching you with the loving eyes of a Father who knit you together sinew by sinew, who knows you inside and out. You may not understand the whys of your life sufferings, but like Hagar, once you realize God sees you, you can be strengthened to carry on fulfilling your purpose. Living with chronic pain has clarified my purpose. Various callings have been eliminated and illuminated, providing a path I do not question. My purpose hasn't been compromised; it's been defined.

THE HEALING POWER OF SIGHT

Jesus, like his Father, saw people. His love drew him to the disabled, the outcast, the hungry, and "sinners." His love and compassion allowed him to see. He looked lovingly into their eyes, communicating their value to him.

We too have eyes to see others through a lens of love that can provide healing for them—to acknowledge those around us who are different, distressed, or lonely. Once we know God sees us, it will strengthen us to see others more clearly. Be strengthened today. The God of love sees you at this moment, and he adores you. Now look to him so you can reflect his love back to those who do not feel seen.

CHAPTER 24

The Gift of Wholeness – The Only One in the World

By Don Talley, Associate VP, Youth for Christ/USA

How can we be whole if we hide behind our pain?

DON TALLEY'S STORY

I was born with a very rare muscle disorder. In fact, when I was seven, after multiple diagnoses and biopsies, I was given the medical status of "unique" as I was the first and only known person with this particular disorder. Similar to muscular dystrophy, the disorder is neuromuscular, causing my muscles to be weak and my body frail. I cannot walk, so I use leg braces for stability and a wheelchair for mobility. I hurt. The disease causes pain throughout my body which comes and goes as it wishes. Although I have found that when I become fatigued, I hurt more. And when I hurt, I become fatigued. Some days become an endless cycle of pain and struggle, which find me longing for purpose and meaning.

My symptoms began as an infant; my family noticed that I struggled to hold my head up while being held. The muscle weakness was most evident in my neck as it just could not support my big head. As a baby, I could not crawl and could only navigate a small area by rolling around on the floor. When I finally got up on all fours, I would assume the bulldozer position, crawling with my head on the floor and powering myself around the house. It worked, except for the rugburns and multiple crashes into walls, doors, and whatever else got into the way as I could not exactly see where I was going.

As a child, I was a regular at the top medical clinics in California, if not the world; UC San Diego, USC, and UCLA all had an interest in examining, testing, probing, watching, and charting my progress. I was a rare and unique discovery, but all I wanted was to be a normal kid. I wanted to run. I wanted to ride a bike. I wanted to surf. I wanted not to be stared at and mocked. I wanted not to hurt. Life expectancy for me was always a moving target. The experts told us I would probably not survive past my seventh birthday. And then I turned seven. Then my twelfth birthday became the expectation. And then I turned twelve.

Along with these prognostications came the dire warnings of the quality of life I could live. It was a busy and confusing time indeed. There were so many doctors and specialists, so many surgeries and experimental therapies but no answers, no solace, and no hope.

THE INVALID AT THE POOL

In John chapter 5, Jesus encounters a disabled man lying beside the pool of Bethesda in Jerusalem. This particular pool was spring-fed, and it was located near one of the ten gates to the city. Specifically, it was near the Sheep Gate, where—you guessed it—sheep were brought into the city. The name Bethesda translates to mean "house of mercy," but to be honest, as I read this story, it feels everything but merciful. The pool had a reputation and a tradition of healing people. At random times, the waters of the pool would be stirred by an angel, and the first person into the water after it had been troubled would emerge healed of their infirmity. Because of this, the pool was surrounded by the sick, the blind, and the lame every day. The man Jesus encountered that day, had been visiting the pool for thirty-eight years. Imagine the desperation and the frustration that grew each day for him and the many people just wanting their circumstances to change.

ELEMENTARY SCHOOL

When I was in elementary school, recess frustrated me time and time again. When the bell would ring, my classmates bolted out the door to the playground. Meanwhile, I began my slow, painful journey to join them. By the time I arrived, teams had been chosen, games had begun, balls had been taken, and inevitably, the bell rang for the next class period to begin, and I began my long return. Day after day, recess after recess, this was my life until one teacher had an idea. A five-minute head start.

Not only did this change the quality of my playtime, but it changed the quality of my social life. My teacher thought it would be appropriate to choose one "helper" to join me for the early dismissal. I became the most popular kid in class. My disability now came with an advantage for them. This went on for years, even through middle and high school.

At one point, the Muscular Dystrophy Association offered to get me my first motorized wheelchair. This would give me much more independence and the ability to navigate school myself. I resisted, explaining to my parents that the social interaction and help I received from my classmates was more important to me than my self-reliance. I was afraid of losing who I had become.

WHOLE

Jesus approached the disabled man by the pool and asked, "Do you want to be whole?" Thirty-eight years of trying to be the first one into the pool. A lifetime of begging for money to make a living. An identity shaped by pain and struggle and disappointment and the daily pursuit of something different. But an identity, nonetheless. Jesus knew that change, even changes that I had hoped for, prayed for, and sought, could potentially be hard. And so, he presented the option.

I have often found that the struggle and pain can become mundane, ordinary, and comfortable in my own life experience. And when it does, I begin to associate my own identity with it rather than seeking God and the potential he has designed for me. I guess it was easy for me to do so because of my unique status. No other person has what I have. No other person feels what I feel. I could look out into a crowd of people and know I would never come face to face with the thing I hated most. It was normal for me to become limited by the circumstances of my life rather than by the freedom of being made whole by the Creator himself. "There is no one to help me into the pool" was an easy excuse for me to hold onto. It gave me permission to hide behind my pain. We certainly are creatures of habit, and sometimes God reminds us that he is everything but mundane.

MELISSA

The phone rang, and on the other end was the most unexpected voice. It was Pam, the mother of a three-year-old little girl named Melissa. Pam went on to say, "My daughter was just diagnosed with your disorder, and our specialist thought we should reach out." The words hung there for a moment while I tried to comprehend what was happening. "Your disorder." For the first time in my life, I was no longer "unique." There was now somebody else in the world who felt what I felt, who knew the pain and struggle of my life. I could no longer hide behind my mirror. I may have to come face to face with the very thing I hated most about my life.

Amazingly, Melissa and her family lived nine hours from my home in San Diego. She was diagnosed by a team of doctors within the same research system I was so familiar with. Her neurologist was a specialist in this field of study and one who had studied my very own muscle tissue. The diagnosis was true and accurate. There was a pull at my heart to go and see this little girl, but there were also some incredibly strong feelings of fear. I was afraid of what may change. I was afraid of losing the life I had built. Finally, there was someone who could help me into the pool, but I wasn't sure if this could fix the brokenness I felt.

After some convincing, my good friend, Rich, drove me to meet Melissa. I was reluctant, unsure, scared, and excited all at the same time. Rich indicated that I barely spoke the whole drive. He knew God was doing something in me. What? We were not sure yet. Nonetheless, we arrived at the house around nine in the evening, and Melissa had already gone to bed. I spent a great deal of the night taking inventory of my life and asking Jesus to show me what was it about this little girl that frightened me so much. I kept hearing his words in John chapter 5: "Do you want to be whole?" I did. Whatever that meant, I did.

In the morning, I could smell breakfast being made and the sound of little feet shuffling across the carpet in the hallway. "When is he going to wake up? I want to meet him!" Melissa's small voice could be heard through the guest bedroom door. As I strapped on my leg braces and prepared to come out of the bedroom, I was overwhelmed with a sense of gratitude and uncertainty.

As I sat on the living room floor, Melissa began to move. She crawled down from her mom's lap and stood holding onto the coffee table. Her thin and frail little body, affected by the disorder, maneuvered around the room toward me. Memories flooded into my head of my childhood. I remembered using the furniture to hold myself steady. I was just as thin and frail. My forehead was scarred from falling, requiring stitches at least twenty times. I hated my weakness. I hated my pain. I hated God for doing this to me. I hated what I had become.

Melissa slowly came to where I was seated and stood for a few seconds. It felt like an eternity. Again, I could hear Jesus asking me: "Do you want to be whole?" I do. Melissa teetered for a moment and fell into my arms. At that very moment I knew God was at work. All my memories rushed through my mind. My anger and disappointment vanished. For the first time in my life, I embraced the little boy in me that was scared, hurt, and alone. For the first time in my life, I actually embraced the very thing I hated most in my life and had tried to ignore for twenty-three years. This was a start to something new; a fresh start to lean into my pain and my struggle and allow God to use the brokenness of my life for his good.

Melissa died at age sixteen from complications brought on by the disorder we shared. We spent many times together during her short life, laughing, learning, and celebrating the goodness of our Creator. Today, at age fifty-four, and after serving in ministry for thirty-three years, I have seen and experienced this truth: to be made whole does not require a physical healing. Wholeness is a spiritual gift that requires us to stop waiting for the water to be stirred and trust the One and only One who will do more than we can ever imagine.

CHAPTER 25

The Gift of Obedience – Humility

If Jesus learned obedience through suffering, how will we?

THE MAN BORN BLIND

As he [Jesus] went along, he saw a man blind from birth. His disciples asked him, "Rabbi, who sinned, this man or his parents, that he was born blind?"

"Neither this man nor his parents sinned," said Jesus, "but this happened so that the works of God might be displayed in him. As long as it is day, we must do the works of him who sent me. Night is coming, when no one can work. While I am in the world, I am the light of the world."

After saying this, he spit on the ground, made some mud with the saliva, and put it on the man's eyes. "Go," he told him, "wash in the Pool of Siloam." So the man went and washed, and came home seeing (John 9:1-7).

It only took once for this man to listen to Jesus—he heard with an open heart even though the experience was a little odd. The man went home seeing because he listened and obeyed.

Now the day on which Jesus had made the mud and opened the man's eyes was a Sabbath. Therefore the Pharisees also asked him how he had received his sight. "He put mud on my eyes," the man replied, "and I washed, and now I see."

Some of the Pharisees said, "This man is not from God, for he does not keep the Sabbath" (John 9:14-16).

The Pharisees couldn't see. Oh, they could see things like rules and rule-breakers, but they would not listen to the opinions of others who were not like them. In their egotistic pride, they fought—even after the fact—against this man named Jesus, who healed the man born blind. The Pharisees kept asking the man how he could now see. The healed man kept repeating his story, but the Pharisees would not take their heads out of their rulebooks to see that this blind man could now see. All they saw was that Jesus broke one of their 613 rules—not to perform work on the Sabbath. They tried to manipulate the man's answer by telling him that Jesus was a sinner and sinful men cannot heal. Jesus, though, never sinned. "If this man were not from God, he could do nothing," said the healed man as he defended Jesus from the Pharisees' accusations (John 9:33).

Jesus further addressed the sinfulness of the blind Pharisees in Matthew chapter 23. I only include three of the "Seven Woes" here. The Pharisees were blind, and Satan controlled them. Jesus addressed the satanic likeness in the Pharisees. Strap on your seatbelt for the "Woes"!

Woe to you, teachers of the law and Pharisees, you hypocrites! You shut the door of the kingdom of heaven in people's faces. You yourselves do not enter, nor will you let those enter who are trying to.

Woe to you, teachers of the law and Pharisees, you hypocrites! You clean the outside of the cup and dish, but inside they are full of greed and self-indulgence. Blind Pharisee! First clean the inside of the cup and dish, and then the outside also will be clean.

Woe to you, teachers of the law and Pharisees, you hypocrites! You are like whitewashed tombs, which look beautiful on the outside but on the inside are full of the bones of the dead and everything unclean. In the same way, on the outside you appear to people as righteous but on the inside you are full of hypocrisy and wickedness.

You snakes! You brood of vipers! How will you escape being condemned to hell?

CONTRAST

In the classic Sermon on the Mount, Jesus told the listening crowds that life going forward would be backward. Before, kings lived in palaces; now, the King is homeless. Before, the Pharisees dictated the behavior of society; now, the love of God would. Before, those who were sick, outcast, and oppressed were on the fringe; now, they would be honored. Before, victory came from winning wars; now, the war would be won by the Savior of the world dying on a cross. It all seemed so backward because it was. It still is. How many people do you know that consider meekness a strength? Or aspire to be gentle? Or strive to obey God instead of following their desires? Jennie Allen writes in her book, *Get Out of Your Head*, "Outside of biblical faith, humility would be lunacy. Who wants less power, less prestige? But within biblical faith, it is virtuous, this utter dependence on God."[46] Eight hundred years before Jesus was born, Isaiah prophesied about the coming Messiah:

The Spirit of the Sovereign Lord is on me,
    because the Lord has anointed me

to proclaim good news to the poor.
He has sent me to bind up the brokenhearted,
  to proclaim freedom for the captives
  and release from darkness for the prisoners,
to proclaim the year of the LORD's favor
  and the day of vengeance of our God,
to comfort all who mourn,
    and provide for those who grieve in Zion—
to bestow on them a crown of beauty
  instead of ashes,
the oil of joy
  instead of mourning,
and a garment of praise
  instead of a spirit of despair.
They will be called oaks of righteousness,
  a planting of the LORD
  for the display of his splendor (Isa. 61:1–3).

Jesus taught this backward way of thinking during his ministry, beginning with the Beatitudes.

Blessed are the poor in spirit,
for theirs is the kingdom of heaven.
  Blessed are those who mourn,
for they will be comforted.
  Blessed are the meek,
for they will inherit the earth.
  Blessed are those who hunger and thirst for righteousness,
for they will be filled.
  Blessed are the merciful,
for they will be shown mercy.
  Blessed are the pure in heart,

for they will see God.

Blessed are the peacemakers,

for they will be called children of God.

Blessed are those who are persecuted because of righteousness,

for theirs is the kingdom of heaven.

Blessed are you when people insult you, persecute you and falsely say all kinds of evil against you because of me. Rejoice and be glad, because great is your reward in heaven, for in the same way they persecuted the prophets who were before you (Matt. 5:3–12).

A humble state of the heart precedes the promises of the Beatitudes. Rewards are not our reason for changing the state of our selfish and prideful hearts, but they are promised to those who do. Suffering is a gateway to benefits from a God waiting to fulfill his promises to those who strive to live a humble life. Suffering humbles us, but Christ embodied humility. Contrast the Beatitudes Jesus taught at the beginning of his ministry to the woes previously listed. Blessed are the people who live *opposite* of the prideful, hypocritical, Pharisaical lifestyle. I think we all agree we'd rather receive a blessing from Jesus than a woe!

How do you honestly feel when you look to embrace the way of life described in the Beatitudes? Poor in spirit. Mourners. Meek. Hungry and thirsty for righteousness. Merciful. Pure in heart. Peacemakers. Persecuted because of righteousness. Insulted. False accusations and evil said against you because of him. Are you willing? These character traits listed in the Beatitudes are not generally respected by the world. But we can be assured, when this earthly life ends, that these attitudes of the heart Satan fights against will be richly rewarded in heaven. God will not say "woe" to you if you say yes to him.

Upside-down. Inside out. Backwards. In this world, we are blind, but the Bible can help us see *if we listen*. The God who sees all does all he can so we also will see. And one day, he will reward us with the promises of the Beatitudes if we change (repent) and become more like Jesus. Turn the camera angle from taking a selfie and instead zoom in on Jesus so you can see. Then you will want to obey. Obedience isn't a word that our pride allows us to swallow easily, but when we do, we'll also go home seeing as the blind man did. Then when we see the power of God, why *wouldn't* we choose to obey his teachings?

JESUS LEARNS OBEDIENCE

Jesus learned obedience to God through his sufferings: "During the days of Jesus' life on earth, he offered prayers and petitions with fervent cries and tears to the one who could save him from death, and he was heard because of his reverent submission. Son though he was, he learned obedience from what he suffered and, once made perfect, he became the source of eternal salvation for all who obey him" (Heb. 5:7–9).

Jesus understands obedience and is entirely obedient to his Father. He desires the same for you and me because of the benefits obedience to the Father provides. I am not preaching a prosperity gospel here; I am backing the biblical obedience and rewards gospel. We cannot be afraid of the word "rewards" in the Bible. If we are, we cannot understand the gospel in its completeness.

- And without faith it is impossible to please God, because anyone who comes to him must believe that he exists and that he **rewards** those who earnestly seek him (Heb. 11:6).
- For the Son of Man is going to come in his Father's glory with his angels, and then he will **reward** each person according to what they have done (Matt. 16:27).

We too learn obedience through suffering because it is most often during suffering that we pray and turn to the pages of God's Word, looking for him and answers to life.

- Before I was afflicted I went astray, but now I obey your word (Ps. 119:67).
- It was good for me to be afflicted so that I might learn your decrees (Ps. 119:71).
- If your law had not been my delight, I would have perished in my affliction. I will never forget your precepts, for by them you have preserved my life (Ps. 119:92-93).

Fellow sufferer and author, Nancy Guthrie writes, "God wants to bring you to a place where you can say, [like Job did after his suffering] 'I've not only heard of you, I've seen you! I know you!' And perhaps he has used pain to bring you to that place."[47]

- My ears had heard of you but now my eyes have seen you (Job 42:5).

CHAPTER 26

The Gift of Light – Good and Evil

How can we appreciate the light unless we've
encountered despairing darkness?

ALL OF US ARE BLIND

"I can't see! I can't see," I kept crying out to my sister, Dawn, in the passenger seat. The winds were hurling their forces against the truck, rain was surging down, windshield wipers were sweeping almost as fast as the winds. The night was as dark as a black hole. We were on I-25 in Monument, Colorado, known for its incessant construction and terrible weather conditions. Traffic was redirected to one lane each way, orange traffic cones shaping the narrow meandering lanes. Few were driving in this hurricane-like storm—but we were. "I want to pull over, Dawn. I can't see!" But we couldn't. I was going too fast and didn't know if I'd be pulling onto the shoulder of the highway or off a cliff, so I had to keep going. Not only was I unfamiliar with driving Dad's heavy Avalanche truck, but I was also in obvious need of a script for eyeglasses.

Leaning forward, squinting, I saw a dim light in the distance. It was pretty far away, and I prayed it was a taillight I could follow. My choices were 1) stop on the freeway and probably get rear-ended and die 2) pull over maybe off a cliff and die or 3) try to stay the course and follow this dim light in the distance, keeping pace and hopefully not die. The dim light was the only sign I had to follow. Dawn was quiet, too terrified to talk. Truth is, she was praying, "Jesus, take the wheel!"[48] We were helpless. We had no choice but to trust and continue through the storm zigzagging ahead. I seriously felt as if I were not driving that truck. I couldn't see! But God gave me a dim light ahead, so I followed.

FEAR VERSUS FAITH

During storms in our lives, it's difficult to know which direction to go. We can't see the future to grab control and make clear decisions. Truth is, we never see the complete picture even if we feel like "I've got this." Calculating decisions is primarily based on our past experiences. We learn from hindsight, but if we keep our eyes transfixed in the rearview mirror, afraid of what lies ahead, we can't move forward. Holocaust survivor Viktor Frankl writes: "The prisoner who had lost faith in the future—his future—was doomed. With his loss of belief in the future, he also lost his spiritual hold; he let himself decline and became subject to mental and physical decay."[49]

The only way to escape fear is through faith. Every day we make faith-based decisions. We trust that when we drive to work, we won't be sideswiped. We might be, but we are more likely not to be, and since we don't know for sure, our decision is based on faith to get in that car and drive. We are trusting. If we don't trust and instead choose to live in fear because we might be sideswiped, we'd never go anywhere. We cannot grow without making decisions based on faith instead of fear. Fear freezes us into doing nothing. We depend on a force outside ourselves to help us see and guide our way.

GOOD AND EVIL

We live in a world of spiritual forces—of good and evil. This world operates in a manner that all of us are blind to. It's called the spiritual realm. In this world there are genuine forces that push and pull at us daily like a monstrous game of tug-of-war. On one side, evil forces can tempt us to lie, cheat, steal, hate, or kill. On the side of good, heavenly forces help us to tell the truth, do our own work, love when hated, or lose our life for another. At work behind the forces of good are God and angels. Pulling us toward evil are Satan and his minion demons. This spiritual world is just as real as the world we see, but it's often forgotten. The opposing forces of good and evil have been at war for our souls since *almost* the beginning of time.

The first verse in the Bible says, "In the beginning, God created the heavens and the earth" (Gen. 1:1). "The heavens" are unseen to the human eye, and "earth" we would soon inhabit. Later in the chapter, after God created light, he created water, sky, land, vegetation, seasons, sun, moon, stars, sea creatures, birds, and animals. Then he created man and woman in his image (Gen. 1:3–27). At some point, probably when God created the heavens, he also created various angelic beings, each kind serving a specific purpose (Job 38:7). The most physically mighty angels are archangels like Michael and Gabriel. There are also seraphs, cherubim, and other heavenly hosts.

The most beautiful angel God created was a cherub, Lucifer, meaning "star of the morning." This was Satan's original name before he sinned against God. God gave him wisdom and the seal of perfection and placed him in charge of all the cherubim—powerful and majestic angels who surround the throne of God and worship and attend to him. No—cherubs are not chubby little naked baby angels with bows and arrows. In heaven, Lucifer was kind of like a lead worship pastor. He was head of the heavenly chorus of cherubs. And he was perfectly beautiful and must have had a remarkable singing voice.

You were the seal of perfection,
    full of wisdom and perfect in beauty.
You were in Eden,
    the garden of God;
every precious stone adorned you:
    carnelian, chrysolite and emerald,
    topaz, onyx and jasper,
    lapis lazuli, turquoise and beryl.
Your settings and mountings were made of gold;
    on the day you were created they were prepared.
You were anointed as a guardian cherub,
    for so I ordained you.
You were on the holy mount of God;
    you walked among the fiery stones.
You were blameless in your ways
    from the day you were created
    till wickedness was found in you.
 Through your widespread trade
    you were filled with violence,
    and you sinned.
So I drove you in disgrace from the mount of God,
    and I expelled you, guardian cherub,
    from among the fiery stones.
Your heart became proud
    on account of your beauty,
and you corrupted your wisdom
    because of your splendor.
So I threw you to the earth;
    I made a spectacle of you before kings (Eze. 28:12–17).

By the third chapter of the Bible, Lucifer had already thought
he was better than God. Even though God created him as one of

the highest-ranked and the most beautiful angel in the heavens, he yearned for *it all*. His heart became proud, and his beauty went to his head. Instead of worshipping God, *he* wanted to be worshipped. Lucifer wanted the cherubim to sing about him, and he persuaded one-third of all the angels in heaven to fight with him to try to take over the throne of God (Rev. 12:4–12). They followed the herd mentality. "Yeah," the demons seemed to have agreed, "let's take God down and become our own gods." Honestly, this mentality is not too far off from where many people find themselves today.

- Those who trust in themselves are fools, but those who walk in wisdom are kept safe (Prov. 28:26).
- For the message of the cross is foolishness to those who are perishing, but to us who are being saved it is the power of God (1 Cor. 1:18).

So, there was a spiritual battle in heaven between good and evil. God had to defend his throne and cast arrogant Lucifer down to earth. God changed Lucifer's "the star of the morning" name to Satan, meaning "adversary," or "accuser." We don't know when Satan's fall occurred, whether hours, days, or years before he appeared in the garden to tempt Adam and Eve. The Bible doesn't specifically say.

How you have fallen from heaven,
   morning star, son of the dawn!
You have been cast down to the earth,
   you who once laid low the nations!
You said in your heart,
   "I will ascend to the heavens;
I will raise my throne
   above the stars of God;

I will sit enthroned on the mount of assembly,
    on the utmost heights of Mount Zaphon.
I will ascend above the tops of the clouds;
    I will make myself like the Most High."
But you are brought down to the realm of the dead,
    to the depths of the pit (Isa. 14:12–15).

And the other rebellious angels (now called demons) were cast from their positions of authority also (2 Peter 2:4; Jude 1:6).

But we have been given a light to follow—God. He may seem like a dim taillight to you now, but you will find it becomes brighter the more you follow and invest time and energy into learning about him. The closer you get to him, the more he will illuminate your path, no matter the darkness you have encountered. "Your word is a lamp for my feet, a light on my path" (Ps. 119:105). The more darkness we've experienced, the more we appreciate the light. And this light gives us wisdom, direction, and hope. "Again Jesus spoke to them, saying, 'I am the light of the world; he who follows me will not walk in darkness, but will have the light of life'" (John 8:12).

CHAPTER 27

The Gift of Trust – Job Never Knew the "Why"

How can we understand trust without living humbly?

PRIDE

Satan's sin of pride introduced sinfulness into the world, for he is the one that tempts us to sin. The first mention of his sin on earth is when he clothed himself as a serpent in the Garden of Eden. Do you know what he said to Eve about the one tree God forbade Adam and Eve to eat from? He slyly hissed, "You will not surely die ... For God knows that when you eat of it, your *eyes will be opened, and you will be like God, knowing good and evil*" (Gen. 3:4-5).

That crafty, slippery serpent tempted Eve to desire the *exact* same prideful obsession he wanted: to be like God, knowing and seeing all. She fell too and slid right into that same slimy snakeskin, and so did her husband. They also desired to obtain *all* the wisdom of God. But God didn't allow them to have it, and with good reason, because humility leads to a godlier life.

Pride is the sin Jesus fought most earnestly against during his earthly ministry, especially with the Pharisees. But heavenly forces pulled that tug-of-war rope across the line for the win against opposing evil spiritual forces, and God remains on his holy throne.

Satan still has power on earth, though. A *lot* of power. In fact, he is sometimes referred to as the "prince of this world" or "god of this age" (John 16:11; 2 Cor. 4:4). God has allowed Satan limited power on earth for a time. But one day, he will be destroyed forever (Rev. 20:7–9). John, an apostle of Jesus, when he was over the hill in age, wrote the final book in the Bible called Revelation. John saw a prophetic vision, and he recorded what was revealed: "And the devil, who deceived them, was thrown into the lake of burning sulfur, where the beast and the false prophet had been thrown. They will be tormented day and night forever and ever" (Rev. 20:10).

"One day the angels came to present themselves before the LORD, and Satan also came with them. The LORD said to Satan, 'Where have you come from?' Satan answered the LORD, 'From roaming throughout the earth, going back and forth on it'" (Job 1:6–7).

That is just creepy.

Satan wants us to be our own gods and join his crew of demons and people disobedient to God's teachings. He roams the earth looking for his next victim to convince them they are self-sufficient, devoid of needing God and his incomparable wisdom. Satan wants us to see things for ourselves with preposterous blind spots and without the help of God. He wants us to rebel against the One who made us and knows us fully. Satan is the "father of lies" and wants us to lie, cheat, steal, and hate. He hates God and wants us to hate him too.

Abdu Murray, in his book, *Saving Truth: Finding Meaning & Clarity in a Post-Truth World*, remarks on this topic; "... in wanting to be God instead of being with God—we have become less than our intended and best selves."[50] Sad truth is that Satan is remarkably successful at promoting self-rule and autonomy over humility and trust in God. But God didn't create us to be above others or to function self-sufficiently. He made us to have a relationship with him and with others. He made us to value other human beings, not promoting ourselves above another or above him.

[Peter said] Be alert and of sober mind. Your enemy the devil prowls around like a roaring lion looking for someone to devour. Resist him, standing firm in the faith, because you know that your brothers throughout the world are undergoing the same kind of sufferings (I Peter 5:8–9).

WHY IS THERE SUFFERING IN THE WORLD?

Satan's disobedience is one reason we have suffering in the world. By causing Adam and Eve to doubt God's instructions, Satan birthed evil. Professor Thomas G. Long from Emory University's Candler School of Theology says, "Sin is the biggest word we have to describe all the powers loose in the world that oppose God's will."[51] Satan tempts us, for example, to commit adultery, slowly searing our consciences: a glance becomes a look, becomes a wink, becomes a secret meeting, becomes a kiss, becomes infidelity. He deceives us one little temptation at a time, so it doesn't feel like a big deal. In reality, our consciences are being seared, so we feel the effects of sin less and less.

The Spirit clearly says that in later times some will abandon the faith and follow deceiving spirits and things taught by demons. Such teachings come through hypocritical liars, whose consciences have been seared as with a hot iron (I Tim. 4:1–2).

JOB

Only God is omniscient (knowing everything), omnipresent (inhabits the entire universe), and omnipotent (his power is limitless). Even though Satan is permitted power on earth, God limits him (Eph. 6:10–16; James 4:7). About the story of Job, Pastor Timothy Keller says, "God allows only so much suffering as to completely refute everything Satan wants to do. God only gives Satan enough rope to hang himself. God only allows enough suffering into Job's life as to actually accomplish the opposite of what Satan wanted."[52]

God knew what he was doing when he gave Satan specific permissions to inflict suffering into Job's life. *God trusted Job.* Isn't that cool that God knew Job would come through victoriously to disprove Satan? "Does Job fear God for nothing?" Satan replied. "Have you not put a hedge around him and his household and everything he has? You have blessed the work of his hands so that his flocks and herds are spread throughout the land. But now stretch out your hand and strike everything he has, and he will surely curse you to your face" (Job 1:9–11). Job cursed the day he was born, but he never cursed God. He still trusted him, no matter his thorns.

When things are taken from us, and we still worship God, we defeat Satan too. Do you trust God as much when you're suffering as when you are not? Do you love God for *who he is* instead of for the benefits he offers? Even though Job struggled terribly, the result was God was proved right, and Satan was discredited. I want God to trust me too. I want to have that kind of relationship with him that my love for him does not fluctuate depending on what he gives me or what he has seemingly taken from me. Like in Job's story, God does not tell us why he allows suffering in our lives. Some of us expect that if God were good, he would give us a comfy life. That is an American tale, not a biblical one.

BEHIND THE SCENES

Thank God he is in this tug-of-war for our souls, along with his angelic heavenly host of angels. He is on our side and is exceedingly more powerful than Satan. Additionally, Satan's crony demons are terrified of Jesus and *obey* Jesus' commands. I know this from reading stories in the Bible of people who were possessed by demons, then freed from them after a sharp rebuke from Jesus (Mark 9:25). I see in Scripture that they recognize and believe in God—they used to be his angels for heaven's sake! If demons believe in God, what other evidence do *we* need (James 2:19)?

We must grab and hold on tight to God's side of the rope and trust him. We are not strong enough to pull it on our own. We need spiritual forces greater than ourselves to win the battle for our soul. We must listen to God instead of luring temptations. We must fight temptation with his help. If we trust him, we can see the unseen spiritual realm better by understanding what is going on behind the scenes. All of us are blind and need guidance to keep our hearts from becoming hardened. Hardening our hearts is a venomous ploy of Satan's, and we are amiss if we listen to his hiss to mistrust the only One who is wholly trustworthy.

Why does God allow suffering in the world? Some things we won't understand until we have a Q&A in heaven. But God is good and has unfathomably more intellect than we, and eyes that see the all-encompassing complexities of the world. We see only a tiny puzzle piece—our own.

CHAPTER 28

The Gift of Adoration – Receiving Love

*How can we feel God's love if we don't accept
his adoration of us?*

GOD'S POETRY

"For we are God's workmanship, created in Christ Jesus for good works, which God prepared beforehand, that we should walk in them" (Eph. 2:10, RSV). The Greek word for workmanship, *poiema*, literally means "God's poetry."[53] In the book *Joyful Journey: Listening to Immanuel*, the authors describe, "Poetry in scripture does not rhyme sounds; it follows the Hebrew pattern and rhymes thoughts. This means that as God's poetry, our thoughts can rhyme with our Heavenly Father's."[54]

> If we live by the Spirit, let us also keep in step with the Spirit (Gal. 5:25).

We can be so close to God that together our lives interlace, like poetry. We can live in the same stanza together as we keep in step, harmonizing beautifully together. Learning that God wants a poetic relationship with me helps me understand that he adores me.

God desires for us to be in rhythm with him, to write the script for our lives artistically with beautiful inflections. Parables are poetic. Psalms are poems that reflect every emotion imaginable. Poetry is sometimes lament, but even there, God is in harmonious relationship with us, hurting with us, rather than dissonate and uncaring. We are in cadence together every step of the way.

RECEIVING LOVE

If love is not freely received, it can only go so far before it is obstructed. Is it easier for you to love God or receive love from him? Do you revel in God's love for you, or do you feel undeserving, not allowing his love to flow into you? He wants you to freely receive his love, to accept his adoration of you.

If you don't forgive yourself for regrets in your life, you block yourself from feeling God's love and adoration of you. He wants to write poetry with you, not a thesis on how bad you think you are. You were created for God's workmanship (poetry). That is beautiful! God adores you! If God has forgiven you, what right do you have to reject the gift of his life for yours? Receive his gift thankfully, revel in it, and you will adore him in return.

The three persons in the Trinity participate in a poetic circle giving to one another and us. Joni Eareckson Tada, in her book *Heaven*, describes how God feels about us:

- As adopted sons and daughters, we are a gift that Jesus and the Spirit give to the Father.
- As a bride, we are a gift that the Father and the Spirit give to the Son.
- As a temple and a dwelling place for God, we are a gift that the Father and the Son give to the Spirit.[355]

We are invited into the Trinity to live poetically. We are in a circle of love with the Father, Son, and Holy Spirit. Isn't that incredible? You can have a poetic relationship with God even while experiencing trials. He is with you, and he adores you. There is space in the *Study Guide for Beauty Beyond the Thorns* for you to try your hand at writing a poem to God.

Worth Waiting For

Lord, even in darkness you are right.
Through suffering you are defined;
Your light silhouettes my soul
With hope.

Even though I battle in the dark
Pain enveloping me,
I'm held
By my creator
Who continues his work in me.

Who is but created once?
Daily you form me—
Sustain me—
Regenerate me.

My heart reaches through the thickness of the dark
To search for what I desire
To know—to see—to love you.
You are my God.

I will not leave you,
And you will never abandon me.

In my weakness
I am held.

I can be patient—
You are worth waiting for.
May my suffering be wasted not
In this love story.[56]

JOSEPH

At the end of Genesis is a story of twelve brothers whose father, Jacob, unfairly favored the second-to-youngest brother, Joseph. Jealous, Joseph's ten older brothers secretly sold him into slavery at age seventeen. In Egypt, Joseph was chosen by Potiphar, one of Pharaoh's officials, and was put in charge of Potiphar's household. Potiphar's wife repeatedly tried to seduce Joseph to go to bed with her, but he refused. He was falsely accused, put in prison, and left there for *twelve years*. But Joseph was far from alone. God was executing a divine plan of adoration for Joseph *and* his eleven brothers *and* all of Egypt.

God had given Joseph a gift of dream interpretation. Pharoah had some disturbing dreams that needed interpreting, so Joseph was his guy. He was taken out of prison, gave Pharoah God's interpretation of his dreams, and became second-in-command of all of Egypt. In response to the troubling dreams of Pharaoh, Joseph implemented a plan to store grain throughout Egypt for the next seven years of plenty for the following seven years of famine.

During the famine, Joseph's brothers came to Egypt from Canaan to buy food. When they arrived, Joseph recognized them, and after some time, he revealed to them he was their brother, Joseph. They were in disbelief, and Joseph said to them, "You intended to harm me, but God intended it for good to accomplish what is now being done, the saving of many lives. So then, don't be afraid. I will provide for you and your children. And he reassured them and spoke kindly to them" (Gen. 50:20-21).

Jacob and his sons and families moved to Goshen and were given the best land to feed and tend their flocks and herds. Jacob and Joseph were joyfully reunited, and Jacob lived in Egypt for seventeen years until he died at the tender age of 147.

People betray us, tell us we are worthless, use us. Joseph's brothers intended to harm him, but God used his suffering for the good of many people, including saving the lives of his brothers themselves. God adored all of them, and Joseph's thorns ultimately brought glory to God because Joseph adored him. We don't know how God will use our suffering for good. But he will. God worked through Joseph's obedience and adoration of him. Like God trusted Job, God also trusted Joseph. God will use your story also to help others know him if you stay in a poetic relationship with him. To endure suffering is a more extraordinary feat than winning a marathon. The finish line of a marathon is only a steppingstone to more remarkable accomplishments for the sufferer. I think Joseph would agree.

CHAPTER 29

The Gift of Empathy – Experiencing the Wilderness

How can we understand the empathy of Christ until we grasp that he himself suffered temptation in every way?

TEMPTATION

When the Israelites were wandering in the desert for forty years, they struggled with three principal things: hunger, putting God to the test, and false worship. Guess which sins Satan tempted Jesus with when he was in the desert alone for forty days? Hunger, putting God to the test, and false worship. Jesus experienced these temptations in the same order the Israelites did.[57] The Israelites fell for the lures, grumbling about the manna and quail God provided for them to eat. They also grumbled about the journey God had them take and so worshipped false gods. They fell for temptations and failed. We fall for these same temptations and fail too.

But Jesus did not. He came out of the desert having suffered but did not fall for the temptation to make bread out of stones. He did not allow Satan to test his allegiance to his Father by throwing himself off a building. And he did not fall for the temptation to be given the "world and its splendor" if he worshiped Satan. Jesus did what the Israelites had not the strength to do, and what we have not the strength to do. But guess what prepared Jesus for his ministry? Experiencing the wilderness—suffering and thorns. Who better to help those hurting than those who have themselves undergone trials? Without experiencing the thorns in the wilderness, we would have no perseverance, empathy, compassion, understanding, joy, courage, gratitude, or deliverance.

What other religion has a god who has been willing to suffer and die a horrific death? Jesus was nailed to a cross, hanging naked for hours in front of the crowds. #MeToo. What other god has done this for you and miraculously risen from the dead? #NoOne. "You see, at just the right time, when we were still powerless, Christ died for the ungodly. Very rarely will anyone die for a righteous person, though for a good person someone might possibly dare to die. But God demonstrates his own love for us in this: While we were still sinners, Christ died for us" (Rom. 5:6–8).

EMBRACE GIFTS THROUGH SUFFERING

Suffering is a gift in disguise. Facing severe trials brings us to a place where no one else can go with us except God; it's a space where only he can fully understand, but this space enriches your relationship with him. Experiencing trials offers opportunities to know God in deeper ways, and what matters more than that? He is what matters, and if it is suffering that draws you two closer together, then count yourself blessed. Heartache sucks the life out of you unless your life aches for Christ. It doesn't mean tears won't flow, but gifts God provides you with during suffering are character traits of himself that will help you climb your Longs Peak. If you are in a season of suffering, your hindsight will show you how he was forming you all along.

Christianity is paradoxical. We live in a "backward economy" in this life. God is chiseling us into an image that looks more like himself. Do not think any longer, like I once did, that people in your life might be better off without you. Do not stop getting up. You will find strength through God's Word, but you have to read it. Keep it in your heart and memorize it for when you are too weak to read. "Keep my commands and you will live; guard my teachings as the apple of your eye. Bind them on your fingers; write them on the tablet of your heart" (Prov. 7:2–3).

If you have a terminal disease and will not get better, you can make the most of your days. Every day you are alive, you have a purpose. You have a chance to go deeper with him; to understand his character, because ironically, God meets you in your suffering to carry you. Let him. Cling to him. Don't fight him, push him away, or get bitter. He empathizes with your pain. He wants you to go to him so he can sculpt you. You can make those doctors' heads turn because of your positivity and faith. His gifts allow you a deeper relationship with him so you can empathize with others to help them have a deeper relationship with him. God is worth sharing. Share him. The strong learn from the sufferings of the weak to help them when their challenges come along. We need one another. God sees you and will journey with you to the day he brings you to your final summit—your heavenly home.

GENNES'ARET

And when [Jesus and the disciples] had crossed over, they came to land at Gennes'aret, and moored to the shore. And when they got out of the boat, immediately the people recognized him, and ran about the whole neighborhood and began to bring sick people on their pallets to any place where they heard he was. And wherever he came, in villages, cities, or country, they laid the sick in the market places, and besought him that they might touch even the fringe of his garment;

and as many as touched it were made well (Mark 6:53–56, RSV).

Power flowed so considerably from the Son of God that people who touched with faith the fringe of his cloak were healed of their illnesses. So, was it a magic cloak Jesus wore, as in a fairy tale? Certainly not! It was even more forceful than a superhero's cape! There is no more extraordinary superhero than the triune God. They have enough empathy to go around. They understand the intricacies of what you are going through, and they will never let your pain be wasted. "May the God of hope fill you with all joy and peace as you trust in him, so that you may overflow with hope by the power of the Holy Spirit (Rom. 15:13).

CHAPTER 30

The Gift of Brokenness – Jesus

How can we find comfort from God in our brokenness
if we don't accept Jesus was pierced for our transgressions?

BROKEN

All of us are broken. We come from broken families with broken hearts, and we grieve broken dreams. We are broken up with and have breakdowns. We barely break even or are flat broke. Our bones break, and our spirits break. Our houses get broken into, and our skin breaks out. We are broken vessels with a broken compass and no clear direction. We wonder when we will have a breakthrough. My brake system warning light has been on for years. I try to decelerate, accelerate, make U-turns, hit the brakes, pound the dashboard, idle, or follow GPS. I need some new brake pads, I reason, but nothing completely fixes my brokenness.

True story: One day, long, long ago, in a faraway land called Nazareth, clouds broke apart to make way for the angel Gabriel to deliver a message to an unsuspecting, humble soul who was told she would carry in her womb a child who would one day heal our wounds. If I were Mary, I probably would have had a major breakdown from the pressure. But thankfully, she chose to look up, endure the scorn of the people, and raise the boy who would become the Savior of our broken world (Luke 1:26–38).

Jesus broke down cultural barriers between the Jews and the Gentiles. He broke stereotypes about who kings are and how they should live their lives and humbly lead their people. Jesus broke Pharisaic rules and their ridiculous, meticulous laws. He broke down barriers with the Pharisees by inviting himself over for dinner. Jesus broke the ranks and did things in a less regimented, more loving way. He walked the broken terrain, breaking in his sandals to show his followers a new way. Jesus hung out with sinners and with those whose brokenness was apparent. He broke walls down between people, speaking of mercy, forgiveness, and love. He broke the chains that bound us to sin. Jesus miraculously healed broken bodies and minds. He broke down and wept in grief over the death of his dear friend Lazarus. Jesus broke out the wine and broke bread with his disciples. He broke down in the Garden of Gethsemane, asking his Father if there was another way. Jesus was broken down, publicly mocked, beaten, spit upon, flogged, stripped naked, and struck on the head repeatedly with a crown of thorns on his head. His naked body was hammered with spikes to logs of wood, then he was put on public display for all to see. There he died, temporarily.

But then, the curtain of the temple tore in two, the earth quaked, tombs broke open, and the bodies of many holy people who had died were raised to life! The hard hearts of the centurion, and those guarding Jesus, broke in despair when they realized, "Surely, he was the Son of God!" Jesus was buried, breaking the hearts of his family, friends, and followers.

And then, Jesus broke out of the tomb, overcoming death to heal our wounds!

Jesus knows brokenness. He understands each brand of brokenness, and he knows our brokenness does not have to be the end of our stories or define us. Life does not end during seasons of brokenness, but it changes us. We can find refuge in the One who broke himself so we can be healed. The benefits of having suffered deliver a superior understanding of the benefits of the cross. We can use our pain to draw closer to him and others. We may try to escape our brokenness by numbing ourselves with alcohol, drugs, food, television, or other addictions, or by hiding in our homes behind the curtains. But we can look to the One who broke himself for us and can relate to our pain. He tore the temple's curtain in two when he died so that all could go freely to him. We don't need to hide anymore.

Jesus had the power to but did not stop the Roman soldiers and others from physically breaking him down. He didn't stop them because he knew *the victory was in the breaking;* the victory was beyond what was physically seen, in the spiritual realm. Reason lies beyond the pain, beyond the thorn, beyond our comprehension. We cannot see what God sees, but if we did, as Timothy Keller says, "... God gives us what we would have asked for if we knew everything that He knows."[58] God sees the benefits of our pain. Our hardest seasons can become some of our most glorious memories and training ground for our future journey. The past will speak for itself in time. Our hoped-for outcome may never transpire, but we can change our perspective to live for what God is producing in us, instead of focusing on our limited view. Give me a nail or a blanket, and I'll choose the nail any day. The cross provides lasting comfort—the blanket, a temporary fix.

FIND YOUR "WHY"

In his book *Walking with God through Pain and Suffering*, Timothy Keller explains, "Suffering is the stripping of our hope in finite things; therefore we do not put our ultimate hope in anything finite."[59] Holocaust survivor Viktor E. Frankl writes in *Man's Search for Meaning*, "We who lived in concentration camps can remember the men who walked through the huts comforting others, giving away their last piece of bread. They may have been few in number, but they offer sufficient proof that everything can be taken from a man but one thing: the last of the human freedoms—to choose one's attitude in any given set of circumstances, to choose one's own way."[60] He also wrote, "... the sort of person the prisoner became was the result of an inner decision, and not the result of camp influences alone. Fundamentally, therefore, any man can, even under such circumstances, decide what shall become of him—mentally and spiritually. He may retain his human dignity even in a concentration camp."[61]

The words of German philosopher Friedrich Nietzche helped Frankl counsel many distraught prisoners in the concentration camps, "Nietzsche's words, 'He who has a why to live for can bear with almost any how,' could be the guiding motto for all psychotherapeutic and psychohygienic efforts regarding prisoners. Whenever there was an opportunity for it, one had to give them a why—an aim—for their lives, in order to strengthen them to bear the terrible how of their existence. Woe to him who saw no more sense in his life, no aim, no purpose, and therefore no point in carrying on. He was soon lost."[62]

Ask God to help you fulfill your purpose. Name the people who need and want you. Find the project (for me it is writing this book) that will help you find the "why" to bear the "how." God has allowed you to be in your circumstance for a reason. If you can be a prayer warrior, you have been given the greatest purpose of all. You matter.

PURPOSE IS THE WAY THROUGH

How can we be overcomers unless we've been underdogs? Finding meaning provides direction in our lives to help us live our life's purpose. If we are to live in the image of God, we are to bear suffering because Jesus did. How do we gain peace? Piece by piece—one moment, one day, one minute, one second at a time.

What do we do when we feel our will is better than his? My will seems safer because it doesn't include chronic pain. But I must remember everything he allows in my life is to lead to one result—the salvation of my soul. I don't have the power to save it. In this pain, I'm sharing in the death, burial, and resurrection of Christ—where darkness meets light. His cross was to die for me, my cross is to live for him. Suffering is the rite of passage to deeper communing with him. He is skimming the dross off me to form me into Joy. El Roi is with me—he sees me.

I don't know if I will ever walk again, but I will always walk with him. I still have a purpose in life; to help others reach out to him in their suffering to experience him—the beauty beyond the thorns. We are broken but have access to a superpower—the Holy Spirit who can guide us through darkness. God understands brokenness, but there is nothing broken in heaven or in the coming new earth. We will be fully healed. There will be no more brokenness or tears, and thank you, God, there will be no more pain.

He was pierced for our transgressions.
The punishment that brought us peace was on him.
By his wounds we are healed (Isa. 53:5).

Conclusion

Summiting Longs Peak

The eastern face of Longs Peak is called The Diamond and is one of the most well-known alpine technical climbs, requiring ropes. It's a tough one. Longs Peak is rated a Class 4/Class 5 climb.[63] Fourteeners are rated by difficulty using "class" ratings. A Class 1 peak is a hike to the summit. Class 2 peaks include sections of "scrambling" where hands are needed to assist with the climb. Class 3 peaks include risky segments of "scrambling." Class 4 peaks include dangerous sections of simple climbing where ropes *are not* used, and Class 5 peaks include sections of technical roped climbing. Class 4 routes are more dangerous than a roped Class 5 climb due to falling, or "exposure."

Without being tethered to Jesus, my climbing partner, I would die from exposure. Someday, together we will reach the top of The Diamond. The treasure hunt I've been on has revealed jewels in unexpected places—through thorns. The Diamond is glamorous but deceiving; greater beauty lies among the thorns. Jesus wore a crown of them and endured exposure for me. He fell, bled, and died so I could one day summit my Longs Peak.

By his wounds we have been healed (Isa. 53:5). "Have been" means his wounds have *already* healed us. If we've responded to his wounding for us and follow his upside-down way of life, all that needs healing already has been. We want our thorns removed, but the pain from the thorns is the very tool that is healing what most needs to be healed in us—our souls. Satan uses thorns to puncture, but Jesus staunches our wounds with himself. His love for us heals us. We have access to his healing love now. No matter the "class" of your suffering journey, it has a purpose.

Seeing God amidst our suffering diminishes the pain, but focusing on fear increases pain. We often suffer more than we need because we dump anxiety, frustration, anger, insecurity, and despair into the suffering cyclone. Our underlying pain is enough, right? We can let Jesus carry the anxiety and fear while we process our primary pain without being burdened with secondary and tertiary pains.

"So do not fear, for I am with you; do not be dismayed, for I am your God. I will strengthen you and help you; I will uphold you with my righteous right hand" (Isa. 41:10). This isn't just a verse to be memorized, it is a truth to be lived. God is with you and because of that, you do not need to be dismayed. God is strengthening you. God is helping you. God is upholding you with his hand. He stretches out his righteous right hand every moment for you to grab ahold of. With his hand he lovingly provides for you direction. With his hands he is "scrambling" for you during your climb. "When I said, 'My foot is slipping,' your unfailing love, Lord, supported me. When anxiety was great within me, your consolation brought me joy" (Ps. 94:18–19).

I am over midway up my Longs Peak. As I carefully turn around to take in the view from this height, I see his deliverance each step of the way. In hindsight I see behind me the obstacles and many days I thought I'd never make it through. I see rocks strewn where I stumbled but where my Shepherd gave me perseverance and pulled me to safety. I see cool brooks where I was led for sustenance. My eyes behold the compass of love and grace that has been tenderly extended to guide me to my True North. I see routes we've taken off the beaten path but have been necessary for my personal growth. I see beauty beyond the thorns because I see him.

> You will go out in joy
>> and be led forth in peace;
> the mountains and hills
>> will burst into song before you,
> and all the trees of the field
>> will clap their hands.
> **Instead of the thornbush will grow the juniper,**
>> **and instead of briers the myrtle will grow.**
> This will be for the LORD's renown,
>> for an everlasting sign,
>> that will endure forever (Isa. 55:12–13).

Looking ahead, The Diamond is in view where the altitude is so high, trees cannot grow. But I know that when we reach beyond the timberline, it doesn't matter the lack of oxygen or the amount of sun exposure I experience, "... for the joy of the LORD is [my] strength" (Neh. 8:10). It matters not what I see, but what my climbing partner sees. His eyes are transfixed on me, leading me in love until the day we summit The Diamond—the day he calls me home.

Until then, we continue our poetic life together writing songs of praise and poems of lament. When it's time to summit The Diamond of Longs Peak, I imagine I will take in the full 360° panoramic view with reverent awe, beholding him complete in his resplendent glory. After he lifts my chin to look into his eyes, I will gaze and gaze and gaze at him forever! He is my beauty beyond the thorns.

Acknowledgments

Thank you, God, for creating space for this book to be written. Space to write was created because of a disability. It's a dream come true to write something that points others to you, my Creator, Sustainer, and True North. You are my best friend.

Mark, I wouldn't be alive without you. You have laid down your life for me, the greatest gift a human can give. You give it with love and sacrifice. Thank you for faithfulness to me and loving me in sickness and in health.

Jenny, thank you for heating up rice bags for your mom since you were so tiny you had to push a kitchen chair to the microwave to climb on it to reach. God saw and smiled. Thank you for warming my heart with your love for God and people. Your compassion is exemplary, and I watch you to learn.

Nicole, your humor and wit since you were tiny have helped lighten difficult moments over the years. "Daddy, you know what your brain looks like? A little piece of gum all chewed up!" Clever little three-year-old. Now at twenty-three years, you are still curious about the brain. I can't wait to learn how your research on physical pain helps those of us who experience it.

Dave, thank you for meticulously reading and rereading my manuscript to help me write more clearly. I am so thankful for the love you have shown me by taking such a deep interest in my life and in my manuscript. The tears you cried and words you spoke after reading these pages will always be cherished inside my heart.

Dawn, thank you for reading my manuscript and crying with me. Outside of Mark you know me better than anyone. After all, I was conceived on your first birthday! I'm so glad as the years go by, we only grow closer. Your love overflows into such generosity, I'm amazed, and want to be as generous.

DaNia, thank you for vacuuming my carpet when you were very pregnant and breathless. And thank you for hosting family parties in your garage instead of up a flight of stairs so I can attend. I love your laugh—it is infectious and healing.

Dan, thank you for washing my hair when I couldn't and for praying with me on the spot for healing when we are together. God sees your tears and hears your prayers.

Rylee, you are a joy to me during a difficult season. I love being your Grammy. You are like a piece of heaven spilling over into my life.

April Alvis, your compassion for my manuscript and keeping my voice intact is why you were chosen as my editor. Thank you for making my words better and for honoring God in your work. Your attention to detail is phenomenal!

Christina Veselak, you are a gifted counselor. God has healed me of many pains through your listening and guidance. This book would never have come to fruition were it not the for the twenty years of talks with you. I have been extraordinarily blessed by your life and wisdom.

Ginger Davis, thank you for stepping in to help Mark take care of me during my first disability. Memories of your compassion, love, and lemon cake still carry me through many tough days.

Thank you to the community of people who have helped Mark and me over decades—there are too many people to name, and many I don't even know. Your love has kept us from experiencing even deeper sorrow and kept all our pieces together. I'm still alive because of your collective efforts. God knows who you are, and so do you. Please accept my profound gratitude.

Thank you to you, for reading the words on these pages. I know you have a story too. There is beauty beyond the thorns for you. Keep seeking God. He is your hope and strength. Through him you will discover gifts of himself within your suffering.

NOTES

Introduction – Ascending Longs Peak

1 John Meyer, "Everything You Need to Know about Climbing Your First Fourteener," July 11, 2019, *The Know: theknow.denverpost. com/2019/07/11/14ers-guide-beginners-colorado/213189*

2 Bob Goff, *Everybody Always: Becoming Love in a World Full of Setbacks and Difficult People* (Nashville, TN: Nelson, 2018), 112.

3 Jen Oshman, *Enough about Me: Finding Lasting Joy in the Age of Self,* (Wheaton, IL: Crossway, 2020), 66.

4 K. J. Ramsey and Kelly M. Kapic, *This Too Shall Last: Finding Grace When Suffering Lingers,* (Grand Rapids, MI: Zondervan Reflective, 2020), 24.

5 Lee Bernstein, *Piggyback Songs: New Songs Sung to the Tune of Childhood Favorites,* (Charlotte, NC: Warren Publishing House, 1983).

Chapter 1: The Gift of Hope – My Journey

Chapter 2: The Gift of Perseverance – Keep Reaching

6 Nancy Guthrie, *Holding on to Hope: A Pathway through Suffering to the Heart of God,* (Carol Stream, IL: Tyndale House, 2006), 55.

7 Guthrie, *Holding on to Hope,* 89.

Chapter 3: The Gift of Compassion – Unexpected Blessings

8 Kenneth L. Barker, "John 5:14, Notes," *Zondervan NIV Study Bible: New International Version,* (Grand Rapids, MI: Zondervan, 2008), 2195.

Chapter 5: The Gift of Love – Better Than a Hallmark Love

9 Augustine of Hippo, *On Christian Doctrine, Book I,* 27-28

Chapter 6: The Gift of Grace – Divine Intervention

10 Gen. 28:10-22.

11 1 Kings 3:5-15.

12 Gen. 37:5-7, 9.

13 Gen. 46:2-4.

BEAUTY BEYOND THE THORNS

14   Matt. 2:12.

15   Lee Strobel, *Case for Miracles: A Journalist Investigates Evidence for the Supernatural*, (Grand Rapids, MI: Zondervan, 2018), 142.

16   Harold S. Kushner, *When Bad Things Happen to Good People*, (New York, Anchor Books, 2004), 129.

17   8.   Jacob Asmussen, "The God Who Heals," March 25, 2020, *Texas Scorecard: texasscorecard.com.*

Chapter 7: The Gift of Courage – He Didn't Run Away

18   Matt. 12:9-13, Mark 3:1-6, and Luke 6:6-11.

19   C. S. Lewis, *Mere Christianity*, (New York: Macmillan, 1960), 118

20   Andrew Murray, *Abiding in Christ*, ed. Jeanne Hedrick, (Bloomington, MN: Bethany House, 2003), 90.

21   Darci J. Steiner, "Courage," 2019.

Chapter 8: The Gift of Joy – Unleashed Gratitude

22   Darci J. Steiner, "In the Black," 2018.

23   2.   InformedHealth.org [Internet], *"How Do Hands Work?",* U.S. National Library of Medicine, July 26, 2018, *NCBI: www.ncbi.nlm.nih.gov/books/NBK83668/.*

24   3.   Ben Fielding and Brooke Ligertwood, "What a Beautiful Name," *Let There Be Light*, (Castle Hill, NSW: Hillsong Music Australia, 2016).

25   4.   K. J. Ramsey and Kelly M. Kapic, *This Too Shall Last: Finding Grace When Suffering Lingers*, (Grand Rapids, MI: Zondervan Reflective, 2020), 216.

26   5.   Jennie Allen, *Get Out of Your Head: Stopping the Spiral of Toxic Thoughts*, (Colorado Springs, CO: WaterBrook, 2020), 153.

Chapter 9: The Gift of Community – Air Pocket

27   Kate Baggaley, "What to Do If You Get Caught in an Avalanche," May 16, 2017, *Popular Science: www.popsci.com.*

28   2.   K. J. Ramsey and Kelly M. Kapic, *This Too Shall Last: Finding Grace When Suffering Lingers*, (Grand Rapids, MI: Zondervan Reflective, 2020), 39.

29   Jennie Allen, *Get Out of Your Head: Stopping the Spiral of Toxic Thoughts*, (Colorado Springs, CO: WaterBrook, 2020), 94.

Chapter 12: The Gift of Mercy – Mr. Miyagi

30   John G. Avildsen, *Karate Kid Part II*, (1986, Columbia Pictures: Culver City, CA)..

31   Avildsen, *Karate Kid Part II*.

Chapter 14: The Gift of Endurance – Purer Than Gold

32   Timothy Keller, *Walking with God through Pain and Suffering*, (New York: Riverhead, 2015).

33   2.   Adapted from Timothy Keller, "My Servant Job," Sermon, *Gospel in Life*, February 10, 2008.

Chapter 15: The Gift of Direction – Dirt Roads

34   Acts 9:4.

Chapter 16: The Gift of Fulfillment – Food and Addictions Do Not Fulfill

35   Franzisca V. Froreich, Lenny R. Vartanian, Jessica R. Grisham, & Stephen W. Touyz, "Dimensions of Control and Their Relation to Disordered Eating Behaviours and Obsessive-Compulsive Symptoms." *Journal of Eating Disorders* 4, no. 1, (2016), doi:10.1186/s40337-016-0104-4.

36   Angela D. Grantham, *Salt, Sugar, Fat: How the Food Giants Hooked Us by Michael Moss*, www.academia.edu./43598975/Salt_Sugar_Fat_How_the_Food_Giants_Hooked_Us_by_Michael_Moss.

Chapter 17: The Gift of Provision – Exponential Multiplication

37   Ted Harvey, "What's the Difference Between the Feeding of the 4,000 and the 5,000?", February 11, 2020, *Somerset Hills Baptist Church: https://www.somersethillsbc.org/shbc-blog/whats-the-difference-between-the-feeding-of-the-4000-and-the-5000/*

Chapter 18 The Gift of a Shepherd – Jesus Rescues Cast Sheep

38   Ian Paul, "The Many Layers of the Story of the Women Bent Double in Luke 13," August 23, 2019, *Psephizo: www.psephizo.com/biblical-studies/the-many-layers-of-the-story-of-the-women-bent-double-in-luke-13/*.

39   Phillip Keller, *A Shepherd Looks at Psalm 23*, (Grand Rapids, MI: Zondervan, 2018), 31 35-36.

40   Keller p. 61.

41   Keller, *A Shepherd Looks at Psalm 23*, 62.

Chapter 19 The Gift of Touch – Lepers

42   Centers for Disease Control and Prevention, "Hansen's Disease (Leprosy)," February 10, 2017, *CDC: CDC.gov/leprosy.*

43   Alan L Gillen, *The Genesis of Germs*, (Green Forest, AR: Master Books, 2007).

44   NIV Study Bible, "Notes," 2 Kings 5, (Grand Rapids, MI: Zondervan, 2011).

Chapter 23 The Gift of Sight – The God Who Sees

45   Jen Oshman, *Enough about Me: Finding Lasting Joy in the Age of Self,* (Wheaton, IL: Crossway, 2020), 49.

Chapter 25 The Gift of Obedience – Learning Obedience Through Suffering

46   Jennie Allen, *Get Out of Your Head: Stopping the Spiral of Toxic Thoughts,* (Colorado Springs, CO: WaterBrook, 2020), 162.

47   Nancy Guthrie, *Holding on to Hope: A Pathway through Suffering to the Heart of God,* (Carol Stream, IL: Tyndale House, 2006), 89.

Chapter 26 The Gift of Light – Good and Evil

48   Carrie Underwood, "Jesus Take the Wheel," Arista, 2005. Written by Brett James, Hillary Lindsey and Gordie Sampson.

49   Viktor E. Frankl, *Man's Search for Meaning, tr. Ilse Lasch,* (Boston: Beacon, 2006), 74.

Chapter 27 The Gift of Trust – Job Never Knew the "Why"

50   Abdu Murray, *Saving Truth: Finding Meaning & Clarity in a Post-Truth World*, Grand Rapids, MI: Zondervan, 20180, 63.

51   Thomas G. Long, *Matthew,* (Louisville, KY: Westminster John Knox, 1997), 98–99.

52   Adapted from Timothy Keller, "My Servant Job," Sermon, *Gospel in Life*, February 10, 2008.

Chapter 28 The Gift of Adoration – Receiving Love

53   E. James Wilder, Anna Kang, John Loppnow, & Sungshim Lop-

pnow, *Joyful Journey: Listening to Immanuel,* (East Peoria, IL: Shepherd's House, 2015), 3.

54   Wilder, *Joyful Journey: Listening to Immanuel,* 3.

55   Joni Eareckson Tada, *Heaven: Your Real Home,* (Grand Rapids, MI: Zondervan, 1995), 292.

56   Darci J. Steiner, "Worth Waiting For," 2020.

Chapter 29 The Gift of Empathy – A Father, a Counselor, and a Big Brother

57   Thomas G. Long, *Matthew,* (Louisville, KY: Westminster John Knox, 1997), 35-36.

Chapter 30 The Gift of Brokenness – Jesus

58   Timothy Keller, *Walking with God through Pain and Suffering,* (New York: Riverhead, 2015).

59   Keller, *Walking with God.*

60   Viktor E. Frankl, *Man's Search for Meaning,* tr. *Ilse Lasch,* (Boston: Beacon, 2006), 65.

61   Frankl, *Man's Search for Meaning,* 66.

62   Frankl, *Man's Search for Meaning,* 76.

Conclusion – Summiting Longs Peak

63   Alex Derr, "What Are the Classes of 14ers? 5 Easy Descriptions," October 7, 2020, The Next Summit: A Mountain Blog: www.thenextsummit.org.

ABOUT THE AUTHOR

Darci J. Steiner has served in the ministry as a teen and women's ministry leader, as well as assisted with church plants in Denver and Los Angeles. In 2001, Darci nearly lost her life after a debilitating fall. During her recovery, she earned her Master of Science degree in Holistic Nutrition and implemented natural remedies into her diet that helped save her life. When Darci became disabled a second time in 2018, she turned her focus toward ministry again by writing her debut book, *Beauty Beyond the Thorns: Discovering Gifts in Suffering* and its companion, *Study Guide for Beauty Beyond the Thorns: Discovering Gifts in Suffering*.

Let's Connect!

Author Website: DarciJSteiner.com
Email: Darci@DarciJSteiner.com
LinkedIn: https://www.linkedin.com/in/darcijsteiner/
Twitter: https://twitter.com/DarciJSteiner
Instagram: https://www.instagram.com/darcijsteiner.writer/
Goodreads: www.goodreads.com/darcijsteiner

Next Steps

- Book an online speaking engagement. Visit www.DarciJSteiner. com for details. In person speaking engagements are limited.
- Recommend this book on your social media sites using hashtag #BeautyBeyondTheThorns
- Recommend this book for Bible study groups, recovery groups, or book clubs.
- Purchase a copy as a gift for a friend that may need hope and encouragement during their trial.

Please Write a Review on Amazon!

Would you consider leaving
an honest review on Amazon for
Beauty Beyond the Thorns
and the *Study Guide for Beauty Beyond the Thorns*?

Deeply Grateful,

Darci

Made in USA - Kendallville, IN
89107_9781737603108
09.01.2022 1345